Reflections from the Marriage Table

Reflections from the Marriage Table

Our Experiences of Love in
Marriage, Family, and Ministry

Ron Clark and Lori Clark

WIPF & STOCK · Eugene, Oregon

REFLECTIONS FROM THE MARRIAGE TABLE
Our Experiences of Love in Marriage, Family, and Ministry

Copyright © 2016 Ron Clark and Lori Clark. All rights reserved. Except for brief quotations in critical publications or reviews, no part of this book may be reproduced in any manner without prior written permission from the publisher. Write: Permissions, Wipf and Stock Publishers, 199 W. 8th Ave., Suite 3, Eugene, OR 97401.

Wipf & Stock
An Imprint of Wipf and Stock Publishers
199 W. 8th Ave., Suite 3
Eugene, OR 97401

www.wipfandstock.com

PAPERBACK ISBN: 978-1-4982-9811-7
HARDCOVER ISBN: 978-1-4982-9813-1
EBOOK ISBN: 978-1-4982-9812-4

Manufactured in the U.S.A.   NOVEMBER 1, 2016

Contents

Acknowledgments | VII

Introduction: Why Use a Table? | 1

Chapter 1   Come to the Table | 5

Chapter 2   What Do We Bring to Our Table? | 22

Chapter 3   Table for Two | 37

Chapter 4   Sharing at a Table for Two | 48

Chapter 5   Filling the Table | 64

Chapter 6   Stories and Ministry from the Table | 72

Chapter 7   Adding a Leaf | 90

Chapter 8   Do We Need a Bigger Table? | 101

Conclusion   May We Be Excused? | 107

Bibliography | 109

Acknowledgments

W<small>E WOULD LIKE TO</small> thank our family and friends who have walked with us through many decades of marriage and ministry. Over the years we have had couples mentor us in the hard questions we had for our family and as a couple. We have had couples model how to walk with Jesus, lead a church, and keep our home peaceful and safe. We have had adult children from ministry families offer us support and advice with our children and each other. We have had many, many others support us in ministry and bless our relationship.

We are very thankful for all of you.

Ron and Lori Clark
Agape Church of Christ
Portland, OR

Introduction

Why Use a Table?

W‍HY DID WE CHOOSE a table for our metaphor of marriage? When we began working on this book we shared with couples the title and found that most thought it was not only an odd choice, but one that aptly described us, our marriage, and our families. As we discussed our plan for the book we found positive feedback not only with this metaphor, but with the hidden meanings that couples began to discover in their own "marriage tables." We realized that the most common metaphor for marriage was a bed, an institution, or sometimes a "bond." While these images have important value, we found that hospitality and sharing a meal together were missing from the daily routines of many families. We also know that all marriages can have a table no matter where the location. The table is ripe with memories, traditions, and symbols that every family can share and adopt to their own style.

We are writing this book for those who want to strengthen their marriage, begin a marriage with a positive direction, or reinforce what is happening already in thousands of homes across the globe. Since we are Christians, we have targeted those who are disciples of Jesus, who feel attracted to the principles Jesus taught over 2000 years ago, or who have a faith in God. As ministers we hope that those in ministry can find something to help as they seek peace and safety in their homes. Whether you are younger, older, are beginning your marriage, have been married decades, or are in a second or third marriage seeking to grow closer to your spouse, we hope that this book helps you in that desire.

At the end of each chapter are discussion questions for you to not only answer but also involve your partner. This book can be used for a small group discussion, a couples' devotional, or a class curriculum. The questions are there to encourage you to reflect on what you are reading and grow with your partner.

There are terms that we use throughout this book. We understand that not everyone has the same understanding of marriage, faith, or some of the teachings of the Bible. We also know that there are words that can be politically charged and have negative connotations to some readers and yet be understood differently by others. We would like to explain some of these to help you as you read this work.

- *Sacred*—This is a Bible term that relates to something "holy," "spiritual," and/or in the presence of God. Its root meaning in the Bible was something that was not common but devoted to or given to God. It usually refers to something we treat with reverence, respect, honor, and tremendous spiritual value. We use this term to suggest that something is of ultimate value to our families.

- *Shalom/peace*—This is a Hebrew term that is more than peace, which many believe simply means an absence of conflict or just a quiet space. God's idea of Shalom or peace was justice, righteousness, safety, rest, healing, and a place where others could be treated with honor, respect, and dignity. Sacred and Shalom are similar concepts as they offer the same peace to humans.

- *Complement*—*Complement* sounds similar to *compliment*, which suggests "saying nice things to others," but has a different meaning. Complement means to complete, partner, or mirror one another so that we can be united and build on each other's strengths. We also believe that this best describes the relationship that works as a team.

- *Submission*—This term is not "obedience" nor is it "unquestioned support." Submission is a willing choice to support another who is leading or involved in a mission. Submission says nothing about status, as in the Bible those of higher status submit to others who are not their leaders. Submission is a willing choice that someone makes. It is not forced. Submission also has the same meaning as respect. To submit to someone means to support, respect, and encourage another who is trying to get a job done. Submission is not possible with a corrupt, dishonorable, or evil person because to submit to someone of that character violates God's plan for all humans, who are to be valued and treated with respect by all individuals. Submission cannot be forced, demanded, or a product of manipulation. Submission is an act of love that is met with love.

- *Mutual submission*—We use this term often throughout our discussions. Unfortunately we have dealt with many, many individuals who feel compelled to enforce that the Bible teaches others to submit to them. Overwhelmingly women and wives are the objects of these discussions. However, we not only believe that the Bible teachers "mutual submission" where both respect, love, and support each other, but we believe that this concept is not taught enough in our churches, marriage groups, and to Christian leaders. Marriage involves "both" individuals supporting, submitting, respecting, and serving each other.

- *Spouse/Partner*—We use these two terms interchangeably because we know that we are working with couples who are married, engaged, or dating. We feel strongly that being a team and complementing each other helps to develop a partnership, and we wish to emphasize that by using the term "partner" often. This is not to suggest we do not support marriage, but encourages us to move past the "spouse" term and see each other as partners in a team seeking to grow stronger and healthier.

As you work through this book, we hope that these terms help you to understand the direction and the questions at the end of each chapter. There may be many other terms that we missed or need to define, but we encourage you to contact us if you need more information, help, or have questions. Most importantly we hope you enjoy reading this and developing your own marriage tables with as much happiness as we have had.

1

Come to the Table

I will create a helper to complement the man ... (Gen 2:18)

Lori Dayton Clark

I WAS BORN MARCH 4, 1967 in Chillicothe, Missouri. My dad was a meat cutter (butcher) and my mother worked at home. I was the youngest of three girls. I was twenty years younger than my older sister, Linda, and thirteen years younger than my other sister, Pam. I was definitely the baby of our family!

I grew up in the same home where my dad was born and my parents married. There was much history in our house. I remember very little about living with my sisters. Linda married when I was ten months old and I became an aunt at age two. My middle sister, Pam, married when I turned six. I loved to stay with both of my sisters. In some ways I always felt special by having siblings whom I could spend time with at their homes!

My dad was the eleventh of twelve children. All of his older siblings would tease him and his younger brother suggesting that they were spoiled because they were the "babies" of the family!

Being the youngest myself, I understood. However, I truly loved hearing stories of how my grandparents always made room at their table for another plate if someone needed a meal. Their house was close to the railroad tracks and there would always be "hobos" (as they called them) that would come to their door. Even if they had little to give, they always found plenty to share. My grandparents passed away years before I was born, and I wish I could have met them. However, the stories lived on through their children! My dad had four brothers; two were confirmed bachelors and built a house next door to the family home. I was very lucky to grow up with these two uncles who lived so close. In my younger years I thought they were only there to take care of my every desire. They loved to spoil me and would always have a treat for me. My older uncle, Glen, loved to cook, and it was delicious. He had been a cook in the army and knew how to make many different dishes. My other uncle, Ed, had a special way of popping popcorn that to this day our family misses! He used bacon grease and popped the corn on the stovetop. These men were gruff and rough around the edges, but they nurtured me. Glen was a bricklayer and Ed worked on the city road-construction crews. I would spend many days talking to them and watching them in the kitchen as I sat at their little table.

While my dad's family was my extended family, my mom knew very little about her own relatives. Her father immigrated to America in 1920 from Switzerland and met my grandmother on the ship. After my mom was born, their marriage ended and she was placed in many different "foster type homes." Unfortunately these would be work farms for children. Sadly she rarely talked about this time of her life. My sisters and I assume she was horribly mistreated. She would often express how thankful she was for the Dayton clan because they took her in and treated her like everyone else! My mom is one of the kindest, softest spoken, and loving persons that I have known. She decided a long time ago that she wouldn't treat her children the way she was treated.

My mom didn't have a job outside the home or learn to drive a car until I was six. She had always worked at home and depended on my dad to "give" her money to buy groceries or have her hair done every Friday. My dad could be very controlling in these areas. He would make her ask every week for money and consistently question her as to why she needed it. She gained a lot of independence when she started driving and working at our high school cafeteria.

The house where I lived wasn't very big, but it had a large kitchen with a long history. This is where everyone seemed to gather. We always ate our meals at the table. During holidays, when everyone was scurrying around, there were always some that sat and visited while others prepared the meal. When it was time to clean up, the same thing happened. Any time you came home, someone was sitting at our kitchen table. My dad always had a deck of cards lying nearby. He would play solitaire while most of the grandchildren would sit by him and play along. He usually gave his opinion and sometimes feelings would get hurt! But, it wasn't about the game, it was about spending time at that table.

My parents taught me hospitality around that table as well as our outside patio picnic table. I learned my love of hospitality from both my parents. My mom did the inside cooking, but when it came to the outdoor entertaining, my dad was king! His sons-in-law would often tease him about how they could make something better... but we all knew his would be the best. We always seemed to have a yard full of people enjoying their cookouts and summers are some of my favorite memories while growing up. I also learned that there was always enough food and always room for one more.

I wanted to pass this tradition on to my children. We have worked hard to eat at our table and invite people to join us, so that our boys will witness and one day practice this. When I picture my past, it usually has some memory of sharing food. As my sisters and I review old photo albums, the table is usually a prop in the pictures and begins many long discussions.

Ron Clark

In 1962 I was born on an Air Force base in Missouri. My father was a captain, pilot, flight instructor, and flew a B-52 bomber plane in

Vietnam. My mom was his second wife and was "an officer's wife." I spent the first eight years of my life moving from base to base because my father was in "Strategic Air Command." We traveled throughout the Midwest United States while he was stationed in Nebraska (where my brother was born), Texas, South Carolina, Kansas, and Missouri. We were like many military families during the Vietnam War era. I would come home from school and see a moving truck with men packing up our house. We would leave the next morning and eventually arrive somewhere new. I didn't mind changing schools two to three times per year. I learned to make friends quickly. I have many great memories of the different schools, bases, and friends I would quickly make during these first eight years.

One image I remember vividly from this period of my life was the "dinner table." The table was where we ate all of our meals. It was where we talked about what was going on in my life. It was where I discovered my favorite foods and dishes that my mom made. It was where we were taught manners, learned to listen, and met new people who visited our home.

While we lived in Abilene, Texas my dad was deployed to Vietnam during 1968–69. My mom had to raise two difficult boys and try to keep her sanity, faith, and emotional balance while my dad was gone. She worked part time, met with the support group called "Waiting Wives," and hired a sweet older lady named Mrs. Hail to care for us (my brother and I called her "Mrs. Hell"). I remember Mrs. Hail teaching my brother and me to cook our own egg omelets, grilled cheese, and grilled PB and J sandwiches. We would fix our breakfast or lunch and eat together. It was the same table where my mom, brother, and I would eat.

My mom drug my brother and me to church, in which we were sometimes kicked out of class for our behavior. The pastor, Grantlin Groves, would visit our home and pray with my mom and us. He gave me my first Bible. We lived in a small apartment and had a small table in the kitchen. It was there where I would see him sitting with my mom with a cup of coffee and his Bible.

Come to the Table

When my dad returned from Vietnam he retired from the Air Force. From 1970 until 1978 we moved only four times. These moves again were in the Midwest—Texas, Minnesota, and Missouri. During my junior year in high school we settled in Missouri where I lived for many more years. Both my mom and dad went to college to finish their degrees, raise my brother and me, and worked jobs to support us. As a retired captain, my dad had a pension, family insurance, and a stipend to attend college. We were able to live relatively normal and stable family lives. When I view photos and home movies of our family during this time of my life, the dinner table seemed to be a common image. We always celebrated birthdays or special days at this table. Since my dad was disconnected from his family and my mom was an only child, all holiday meals were four to six people (if my grandparents came to visit), and occurred around the table in our home. My brother and I didn't know what a "kids table" was—we always ate with adults. Sometimes we had two tables—a kitchen table and a large "dining room" table in our home. Most of the time we ate at the kitchen table since it was small and we could visit more. The dining room table was for special occasions and we were expected to dress nicer and use our manners.

The table was the one stable element for my family. We ate hundreds of meals at these tables. We celebrated holidays, birthdays, and special days around the table. Guests, flight school students (some who later died or went missing in action in Vietnam), officers, kids, families, relatives, neighbors, and friends joined us at the table. News was shared at these tables. Manners were required at the table. We couldn't answer the phone during a meal because, "If it's important they will call back." One had to ask to be excused and being told to leave and go to bed without supper were punishments from this "sacred place."

Once my dad called my wrestling coach and told him I couldn't keep my head up at the dinner table because I had cut too much weight—therefore I was to wrestle at a heavier weightclass. It completely floored my coach—no one had done that before. I was mad and didn't talk to my dad for a couple weeks, but when

9

I became a man I thanked him for caring so much about me. You had to be present at the table both mentally and physically. Eating and talking at the table were serious things and probably the only time plans could be made.

When I left home I found the table to also be a common thread in my life. While the cafeteria tables at the university were larger and more impersonal, there were many times when a meal would last an hour or more as my roommate, cross-country and track friends, or other classmates ate together. We would visit, gripe, joke, or talk about an issue well past the closing of the serving line. Later, when I became a Christian, these tables were a great place to talk about faith, doctrine, or pray for each other. In the summers I worked for the Missouri Conservation Department with two friends and lived in an apartment. We would also spend hours at the table talking after we fixed dinner. I now realize how the table had become such a subliminal image for me because it represented more than food!

I realized that things were different in my family when I returned home to visit on breaks or holidays. My mom would tell me that she missed my "eating her cooking." My dad would say that "One fourth of the family left and our food bill was cut in half." My brother became picky in his eating. They ate at different times and sometimes different places. My last two years of high school my dad had begun saying, "No more talking about sports at the table." During college breaks, as a biology major, that ban included biology and chemistry labs. Things had become different in my home. Within a couple years my brother would be kicked out by my dad and joined the Navy. My mom and dad separated and later divorced. I would go home and end up eating out most of the time.

When I was single I took my grandparent's kitchen table, since they had both passed away. I would regularly fix myself a meal and eat at *my table*. I would often invite my youth group, friends from church, neighbors, and dates to *my table* to eat (including Lori who later became my wife). In looking back I don't think I was aware how prevalent this image was for me, or how important it would become. It was a place where I could relax and find peace whether eating alone or with others.

Two Tables Join Together

Our first couple of dates involved the table, although we ate dinner out at other places. A couple evenings before we were engaged we ate at Ron's home. He fixed dinner, which was actually warmed leftovers that one of our church members gave him. The woman was from Taiwan and made the best egg rolls and Chinese food. She gave him extra and asked that he invite a young lady to dinner. The night after we were engaged, Lori fixed a steak dinner and we ate at her parent's table. We had begun to bring the table into our relationship, which continues to be a stable and permanent image in our marriage and family.

Our two tables were similar but different. Like our family histories our tables represented who we were. Lori's was oak, while Ron's was particle board with an oak veneer. Lori's family went to church and were active in the local congregation (where Ron was a youth minister). Ron's dad was an atheist, and his mom took the boys to church as much as they would let her. We were both active in youth groups. We both did what normal teenagers did, which includes some rebellious behavior along with respectful behavior. Ron's family were more "white collar" and college educated, while Lori's family worked blue collar jobs. Her parents had been married forty years while Ron's were just divorcing (after twenty years of marriage). Lori's dad was a butcher and had served in the Army during World War II, while Ron's dad was a clinical psychologist and retired from the Air Force after his tour in Vietnam. Both of us remember our mothers being questioned often concerning how they spent money.

Our marriage involved more than just adding another leaf to the table or pushing two tables together to make a bigger one. It was not that simple. Our tables were unique, similar, and sometimes clashed. Our marriage involved more than simply putting a tablecloth over both (to hide the two styles) or buying a new table and throwing the old ones away. These tables were who we were—good and bad. The legs did not match, the veneer was completely different, and one was taller than the other. Yet these two tables came together to form one family.

Both tables were solid, dependable, useful, and well worn. They had rich stories and traditions that needed to be blended and told in their contexts. They represented the best in both of us, our families, and our futures. When we married, we had to find a way to combine these tables into a new image, one that would be ours.

The Two Become One

In the early story of creation God created male and female as *complements*. In the text, often read at weddings, the story of creation is intriguing.

> There was no helper to *complement* the human. Yahweh God caused the human to sleep; and took one of his ribs/side and then closed up the place with flesh. Yahweh God made a woman from his side and she was brought to the human. The human said, "This is bone of my bones and flesh of my flesh; she is called 'woman,' since she was taken out of human." That is why a man leaves his father and mother, is united to his wife, and they become one flesh. Adam and his wife were both naked, and they felt no shame. (Gen 2:19–25)

This is a story that we often use in premarital counseling with couples, as well as when we speak concerning marriage. While we often hear this text read at weddings or used to discuss the institution of marriage, it has more to offer than just a simple story concerning the origin and establishment of marriages.

Helpers Who Complement

First, the word usually translated *helper suitable* or *helper fit* is a Hebrew phrase that suggests the couple are *helpers who complement each other.* It is used in the Hebrew Bible for a country that is south or opposite another, a region that lies in front of a different one, or something that is a mirror image. A form of the word for complement is also used for a leader. This word indicates that someone is in front of another, or in their presence. This is not to suggest that males and females are opposite, but that they *complement* each other. We have chosen to use the word complement because we understand, from this text, that male and female complete each other. This suggests to us that the two become a team, united, and partners who "add to" or "enhance" one another in this relationship (which explains why the Bible indicates that they cleave to each other and become one). We suggest that couples who complement each other do not see their partner as "lesser" or "greater" but seek ways to support one another in their relationship and what they accomplish as a team. Each one offers something unique to their marriage. What we each provide can enhance this relationship and help each other to mature and develop spiritually and therefore, each individual should be valued and respected. This is what we mean by complement, team, or partner in the marriage.

Rather than standing in opposition to each other, the two blend, and are united. They become a team. Thus the statement from the author of Genesis, that because of this a man can unite to his wife, means that they *complete* each other. Eve provided what no animal could provide for Adam—she became his partner. Both spouses provide what the parents provided and offer emotional support, guidance, love, and acceptance. In marriage males and females are not opposites (as in "opposites attract") but *complement* each other. "Be assets, not liabilities. When we learn to maximize our differences for the benefit of the marriage, we align our lives with God's purposes. The Bible calls this marital unity."[1]

When we discuss this passage with couples we encourage them to go home, talk about the story, and share together how they complement each other. This is important especially for men because they need to understand that their spouses not only complete them but partner with them as a team. Women also understand

---

1. Chapman, *Four Seasons of Marriage*, location 1933.

that their spouse should welcome their contribution to the marriage as well. In this context, marriage is a team effort. Both have strengths and vulnerabilities. Over the many years of working with couples we have found that individuals may be different, but when they partner in marriage they both complement each other. In the past males were less communicative, found self-worth through their work, and struggled to express love and support. Females, we found, seemed to be expected to be more adept at sharing feelings, stay home with children, and regularly provide love and encouragement in the relationship. Now things have changed and people are adapting to that change. Traditional roles have also adapted. We now experience just as many males who are open, communicative, and comfortable staying at home to raise their children, as we are females who tend to struggle to communicate and desire to find a career. However, today many marriages struggle not because roles are changing, but because couples are not encouraged to see their relationship as a partnership and one that complements the other. As Sells and Yarhouse suggest, "To be married is to exercise the give and take of being sufficient for another and permitting another to be sufficient for you."[2]

Our first few years of marriage were tough, as it is for many people. We spent less time learning how we complemented each other and more time struggling to be right. This struggle to be better or right became less about our partnership and teamwork and more about getting our way. As individuals we worked to achieve independence. As a team we struggled to be independent of each other. When couples do this they add stress to their relationship. This stress and striving for independence pressure the couple to create rigid roles. If they were raised with traditional roles (men/fathers work and are public, women/mothers stay home and are more private) they may try to force each other into this preconceived role. These roles in the relationship become defined by outside standards, beliefs, and cultural norms rather than what is best for the "team" couple. The roles also become rigid and the team is not able to remain flexible and adapt so that they can face many

---

2. Sells and Yarhouse, *Counseling Couples*, 60.

diverse circumstances that people experience. Their relationship becomes a competition instead of a relationship of love, respect, and joy.

- Couples who compete with each other can develop behaviors that become controlling, manipulative, and sometimes oppressive. Many times one of the individuals becomes the main controlling partner and finds satisfaction in continually winning. The other develops coping skills that cause them to overfunction. This competition robs each partner of the ability to complement the other, and because of this they adapt, many times in an unhealthy manner. One person realizes that they can underfunction and achieve both control and satisfaction, while the other overfunctions and works to save the relationship. *This is exploitation.*

- Couples who compete can develop individual identities separate from the marriage that cause them to become selfish and seek self-gratification. As time progresses they think more as individuals than a team. They, like the quarterback who forgets that the center is his protector, credit themselves for the win. *This is selfishness and arrogance.*

- Couples who compete cannot complete each other, because they are always trying to win. One person has to lose so that the other can win. *This is oppression.*

- Couples who compete damage each other's self-esteem, and teach the rest of their families that relationships do not involve sharing, mutual respect, and support. *This is dysfunction.*

- These marriage tables become "dinner for one" or an empty expression of a lonely house. They sometimes become a place where one serves their spouse, like a waiter. Like a large table in a cold dark dining room, these tables are avoided by families and hold strained tense family dinners. People ask to be excused quickly, because no one wants to eat there.

The biblical text teaches that male and female work together to help each other become better. We no longer need our parents because we have each other. Parents have the responsibility to complement each other in their marriages so that their children will mature and seek a complement in their lives, as they saw it in their parents. To those who complement each other, marriage becomes a place of maturation, growth, and healing. Their tables are full of fruit, healthy conversation, respect, and love. The table becomes the place to be, and families look forward to gathering around this sacred furniture.

We Are Both Humans

Second, *males and females have the same origin.* They originate in humanity, which was created by God. Just as women give birth to life, so women came from men's side. Both have each other to thank for life. Both depend on each other for existence. Both need each other to live.

While there has been much written concerning the differences between the male and female mind, behaviors, or physical being, the truth is that both are human. As humans we develop, mature, transition, adapt, and survive. In the past we held to the belief that "Men were from Mars and Women were from Venus." Gottman and Silver indicate that males and females equally find sexual and emotional satisfaction in a relationship where there is a high quality of friendship between each other.[3] In reality we are earthlings, and while we share the same planet we have much in common as humans. We are also vulnerable as humans, and need community, partnership, and support. What one partner needs in the marriage is what the other needs as well. *We all* need love, we all need respect, *we all* need to communicate, and *we all* need encouragement. Male and female are both in God's image and marriage is a complementing relationship where both can become like God. This also leads to a satisfying and loving marriage.[4]

---

3. Gottman and Silver, *Seven Principles*, 17.
4. Ibid.

Since we are both in God's image it is important that we remember that God is our individual source as well. Our relationship with God is strengthened when we are in harmony with our spouses. Clint and Penny Bragg, who reconciled their marriage after decades of divorce, have heavily stressed that their reconciliation with each other paralleled their reconciliation and relationship with God. "Many people fail to see the correlation between the quality of their relationship with God and their marriage. We too were once blind to that connection. But during our years apart, each of us developed the deep spiritual roots we hadn't put down as young converts. And God showed us how the intimacy we cultivated with Him directly affected everything else in our lives, especially our relationships."[5] Even the Apostle Peter stated that a husband's relationship with his wife would affect his prayers and relationship with God. "Husbands live considerately with your wives, who are the more vulnerable vessel, so that nothing will hinder your prayers" (1 Pet 3:7).

Partners and Friends

Third, *woman was taken from man's side to be his partner and friend*. In America, we live in a country that still devalues females. This encourages competition, oppression, self-centeredness, and dysfunction. Males who do not partner with their spouse suffer because they become deficient. Males and females were created to be a team, not competitors. In the Genesis account, males and females were both human and in the image of their God. Males and females can view each other as a partner, rather than a threat, and both are able to support each other by valuing each one's individual gifts created by God.

In this story not only is there a lesson for marriage but society. Males and females share much more in common than we would like to admit. We cannot complement each other if we are pointing out our differences and weaknesses. To treat one as the

---

5. Bragg and Bragg, *Marriage on the Mend*, location 502.

weaker sex only breaks down the team. We all bring strengths to the marriage table, and these strengths are celebrated in the shared meal and discussion. They should also be used to enhance our relationships. Our weaknesses can be strengthened when we choose to *complement* rather than *compete*.

Trust

Finally, *marriage is a relationship of honor, vulnerability, and trust*. The biblical author suggested that both were naked and not ashamed. The word for naked (*arum*) again appeared in Genesis 3:1, "and the snake was shrewder (*arum*) than all the other animals . . ." Nakedness is vulnerability and can be something beautiful or exploited, creating shame. The snake represented evil because it brought shame to their relationship. Satan introduced competition to both male and female. Marriage is a relationship where two people can be open sexually with each other. It is a covenant where they can be vulnerable with each other and enjoy the nakedness of their relationship. Marriage is a partnership where sexuality is not shaming or untrustworthy. Nakedness in marriage is honorable when it involves trust, respect, sympathy, empathy, and love for each other.

Trust also requires us to be vulnerable to others. This is especially true when one who has been hurt through unfaithfulness or exploitation attempts to enter a relationship after the pain of the previous one. The fear, pain, and lack of trust can cause us to create emotional barriers for protection and keep us from being hurt again. If someone in our marriage hurts us, we might attempt to move past the event by refusing to become vulnerable again. However, this is not love. Love is manifested by a God who died on the cross, as well as one who took care of Adam and Eve when they sinned and reestablished a relationship with a world that was flooded due to sin. Jesus also developed friendships with some who betrayed him and came close enough to humans to be murdered on the cross. However, our model for love is one who teaches us that while trust must be earned, someone still has to offer the chance to earn it. Couples cannot have healthy and loving relationships until they grow closer together through trust. Those who have broken trust must work hard to earn it back, but those who have been hurt must realize that a relationship will never happen until someone is willing to trust.

This is why sexual infidelity, pornography, and sexual dysfunction can bring such pain to a relationship. It destroys trust and it introduces shame. It creates tension and guilt. It exploits the vulnerability of the complementing partnership because each individual needs to be encouraged to believe that their teammate has their back as well as their best interest. It creates emotional distance between the couple, both sexually and relationally.[6] Too often we hear young people state that they will live with their partner rather than marry them because, in their words, "marriage is fighting, slavery, and oppression."

They have the wrong view of marriage.

We wonder where they learned this view.

Couples who have experienced divorce or pain from a previous relationship may carry this mistrust, hurt, and fear into their next marriage or relationship. It is important to participate in counseling and/or premarital counseling to address this pain as it can be projected onto the new partner. Joining a "new team" is more complicated than simply having a "better attitude" or hoping that "this time around I will be happier." What we experience stays with us and we must be careful that we don't let the pain and unresolved issues from the past live on in our next relationship. Counselors are skilled listeners and able to coax people into taking risks and yet, while still protected, learn to value each other in relationship.

The marriage table is a powerful metaphor for a couple, who are vulnerable and naked but not ashamed. Many times food and body image are linked to nakedness and shame, yet the marriage table is a place where males and females are supposed to accept and complement each other. Cooking and preparing food together can be sexy! Rather than commenting on each other's body size and food intake, the marriage table is a place to celebrate that

---

6. Gottman and Silver, *What Makes Love Last?*, 62–64.

we not only need food, but we need to share food. To be naked and unashamed is to be vulnerable and feel valued, trusted, and respected. The marriage relationship offers this acceptance, love, and support. As we grow older and mature we realize that we are in love with our partner and it is them we want to make love to, not a body or flesh. The marriage table is the place where we open up and become vulnerable, yet it is also the place where love is expressed and trust is affirmed.

Our Tables

When we brought our tables together we had no clue what would happen. We knew we loved each other and would work things out. Our tables were unique but different. Little did we know that the tables complemented each other—we had to explore that ourselves, the hard way, and over time. However, over the years we learned that our relationship was more than buying a new table, combining the two tables, or choosing one over the other. Our relationship involved learning from each other, accepting strengths and weaknesses, and complementing each other so that we could be a team that would one day encourage the children to leave and cleave, so that we could return to our table and appreciate its unique character.

For Discussion

1. On a piece of paper draw a line down the center to form two columns. Put one name on the left column and the other person's name on the right column. Each of you list and discuss what you bring to the relationship and how each enhances or complements the marriage or relationship.
2. What is your definition of what it means to be a *complement*?
3. What is the difference between complement and compete?

2

What Do We Bring to Our Tables

The two will become one ... (Eph 5:31)

HUMAN BEINGS ARE CREATED in God's image. In the Genesis account the author quoted God as stating, "Let *us* make humans in *our* image" (Gen 1:26). Notice that God is *we*, and so are *we*. Since God is community, so are humans—assuming that *we* believe that *we* are created to reflect God's glory, image, and nature. If God is *we*, then humans are to exist in community, in harmony, and in relationship. Assuming that God used relational pronouns also suggests that our existence involves relationship. To be alone, lonely, and isolated is, as God put it, "not good" (Gen 2:18).

While the first two chapters of Genesis have been used to illustrate the foundation of marriage, the text also illustrates a powerful message to us concerning community, humanity, and male/female relationships.

- What does it mean to be human?
- How does humanity reflect the nature of the creator?
- How should male and female live together in community?

Long before there were gender roles, male and female lived together in paradise. Can marriages reflect this paradise, this harmony, or this form of community?

The Genesis text also indicates that males and females leave their parents and unite together. If humans live in community as a family, what does it mean to leave that family and begin a new one? If being in community is the goal of God's people, how can humans transition safely to form a new community? Even more, what is it like to live in relationship under the larger umbrella of community?

Healthy Community

First, *we live in community with our close family. Families that love each other provide healthy relationships* that foster trust, support, nurturing, growth, respect, acceptance, and hope. This is love. Love is more than an emotion. Love is a driving force in relationships. Love happens when people feel trusted, supported, accepted, honored, valued, and good about themselves as well as others around them. Therefore, trust and respect must be present for love to grow. Sells and Yarhouse have written that trust is a major component which reflects the health of a marriage. "While empathy serves as a magnetic force that pulls people toward one another, trust is the adhesion that can keep people together. We have found that, though not an empirically based opinion, the question of trust is a better gauge of relational intimacy than the question of love."[1]

Trust is also necessary for a family to develop and mature in a healthy manner. Within families children learn to walk, talk, and be who they are without humiliation, shame, and fear. Families teach others how to love, show grace, forgive, make amends, and develop emotionally, spiritually, and physically.

> Family structure is different from family style. Family style is concerned with how the family comes across to others. It has to do with who appears to be in charge of

---

1. Sells and Yarhouse, *Counseling Couples*, 147.

the family and who appears to be responsible for certain items (maybe in accordance with a particular Christian denomination's tradition). Family structure has to do with the way the family organizes itself around certain individuals. Family structure has to do with who really has power in this family, who really calls the shots. The healthier the family, the less difference there is between style and structure. In a healthy family things are as they appear to be. The greater the differences between style and structure, however, the greater and more powerful the family secrets and dysfunction.[2]

Families provide a safe environment allowing others to be who they need to be. When we leave that family to form a new one, we retain the traits of our family of origin.

Families that love each other teach boundaries. Children learn good touch, bad touch, self-respect, the respect of others, and how to develop healthy relationships. They observe how their parents, siblings, extended family, and friends of the family treat each other, and they typically imitate this behavior. Families allow each other to go to another room to calm down, express their anger, or reflect on their actions. Families trust each other and what will be said to outsiders about them. In a family one learns healthy boundaries, such as the ability to state one's opinion and disagree safely, encouragement to think for themselves, age appropriate choices for each person and training to make choices with safe consequences (not using anger and fear), and an appropriate or safe use of anger in the home.[3] In this environment each person is able to develop to become who God called them to be and mature with a healthy view of self, others, and community. Families respect each other's physical and emotional space as well as their privacy. "You are like you, not someone else," is a healthy boundary. Families give permission to both be alone and in a group. Families respect each other's right to an opinion and choice. We may influence the opinions of others, but that happens because we are trusted, loved, and respected.

2. Cloud et al., *Unlocking Your Family Patterns*, 77.
3. Ibid., 142.

What Do We Bring to Our Tables

Gottman and Silver have indicated that in a healthy marriage (they use "emotionally intelligent") males are open to the influence of females.[4] Each person trusts the other but is influenced rather than coerced to be like their partner. We are influenced by and influence those in our family because an environment of respect flourishes. We become like each other because we value one another.

In the case of blended families, stepparents understand that they can, at best, be close friends of their spouse's children. The children will bond with their biological parents (even if one is deceased) and will struggle to relate to them. Stepparents (while supporting their spouse) can also advocate for the children and develop a relationship that can become unique in that they are both friend, and parent. However, it is always important for stepparents to realize that their spouse's children may use this to their advantage or try to manipulate the couple concerning parenting. They are simply doing what children do, but parents and stepparents can reinforce boundaries and communicate that their spousal relationship will need to be strong and the children should support them, as long as the relationship is healthy and safe.

Adoption is also a difficult issue for parents and children. However, allowing children to have boundaries with their biological family as well as their adoptive family is healthy, while teaching them to develop respect and trust in these relationships will support their growth and development. Siblings in blended families will also have permission to navigate the complex emotions, trust issues, and anxiety that accompanies new families and relationships. Children can never be forced into having relationships but should always be allowed to question, be cautious, and allow relationships to form and develop.

Families that love each other are flexible. Different situations involve differing actions and consequences. Children are not all the same. Families experience trauma, loss, sickness, mental illness, environmental changes, social pressures, and geographical and ethnic transitions. Families work together to adapt and grow in various circumstances. Families sometimes blend, adopt new

---

4. Gottman and Silver, *Seven Principles*, 104–5.

members, and lose members to illness. Because of this families will change. Couples will interact differently from their parents and will raise children uniquely. This will happen because they will realize that teams overcome by adapting and surviving any test they face. In the middle of the twentieth century two psychologists, Murray Bowen and Michael Kerr, proposed that humans' emotional health was best measured by their level of *differentiation*.[5] *Differentiation* was a person's ability to be close to others in relationship, yet feel comfortable being alone. This person in marriage was able to have a healthy relationship with their spouse, yet feel free enough to have friends and spend time with them. The opposing poles of differentiation would either be *enmeshment* (lose your personality in a controlling relationship with another) or *disengagement* (to not be able to connect emotionally with others). Bowen and Kerr indicated that relationships experienced stress because people were fighting for independence, yet seeking to be close. Many young couples struggle for their independence when they are simply trying to be differentiated in a healthy manner.

This means that one can spend time with their spouse, yet go out with friends and have fun. Their partner also feels comfortable with the time apart and is not controlling, yet trusts when the other is out with friends or coworkers. Differentiation is achieved when a relationship involves trust, respect, love, and empowerment. Families adapt and overcome by loving each other through healthy relationships, boundaries, and flexibility.

New and Healthy Communities

Second, *relationships under a larger umbrella mean that families exist relationally by forming new communities.* Males and females leave their parents, cleave to their spouses, and grow closer together. Many who believe that marriage is divine have faith that males and females were created as complements—we were meant to unite and become unique. Unlike our parents we are unique in

---

5. Kerr and Bowen, *Family Evaluation*, 7.

What Do We Bring to Our Tables

that we are distinct from them. Unlike our parents we live in a different time, with different values and stressors. Unlike our parents our desires and experiences are unique to us. However, when two individuals come together they merge their personalities, dreams, hopes, desires, and needs. No longer is it, "What do *I* want?" but "What do *we* need?" or "What do *we* want?"

Our parents were to love each other, develop their unique families, and prepare those who choose to marry to have a healthy and loving relationship with their spouses and others. Once we marry, they become advisors—and their advice is only as good as their history with us. Hopefully our parents worked to show us that marriage was a relationship of respect, honor, value, love, grace, support, and peace. They did this because they loved each other and us. They also did this because they knew that we needed this model for our own relationships. Children raised in emotionally healthy families carry that love and respect into their intimate relationships. When we left and united with our spouses, we had the opportunity to show our parents that we knew how to have a loving relationship. If we have children the cycle continues and we seek our parent's wisdom so that we can guide and nurture our own children. However, it will sometimes be different from our parents' family.

If at any point we did not have that family relationship or example from our parents, we may face marriage with fear, anxiety, and mistrust and respond by controlling (enmeshment/fusion) or disconnecting (disassociation) from others relationally. We bring these weapons to our tables and the war begins. Ron was a teenager in Boy Scouts. When they went on winter campouts they would turn tables on their sides for protection in toilet paper fights. The structure designed for eating and sharing a meal together became a shield. As they hurled full rolls of toilet paper at each other, most hid behind the tables. No matter how soft the tissue was, when a full roll hit you in the face, it hurt. When we bring weapons to the marriage table, the very instrument of peace and love becomes a protective wall, shield, or boundary, while we hurl insults at each other. We hide behind the tables because we feel superior or inferior towards our partner. We wound because we were wounded and we retaliate because our wall was shaken. Our table becomes a shield rather than a safe place to talk, eat, and share our feelings.

Fortunately we live in community where we can actively seek those who use their tables for peace, rather than protection. We look for those who sit at the table, rather than hide behind it. We gravitate toward those who can show us how to eat at our table and welcome others, rather than turn it over and lash out.

New Journey

Finally, *our families should equip us for this new journey*. As we mature we begin to realize that what we learned in the home was what we wanted to have in our families, or something we wanted to avoid. Some go to extremes and try to do the "opposite" of what they learned at home. We must accept that our families have left an imprint upon us. If my family was all bad, what do I do with my tools? How do I know what was good and what was bad—what are tools and what are weapons? Sometimes this causes us to hide who we are from our partners. Other times it causes us to over exaggerate our family of origin issues. Sometimes we fail to acknowledge that our family of origin reflected what we saw as *normal* or *familiar*, and that only time, education, and work will help us to realize that it may have been unhealthy. Then we can overcome these patterns of behavior. Other times we use our weapons to wound, as we witnessed in our own house.

There are patterns of behavior that we learned from our family that were good, but in our new family they seem out of place. Times have changed, women are more comfortable working outside the home, and children have more individualized toys to keep their attention. Change and adaptation are not inherently bad; they are necessary for a team to stay together, grow and fulfill the goals and visions they have set.

What Do We Bring to Our Tables

Lori

I first met Ron at a church picnic. He was the new youth minister at our church in Chillicothe, Missouri. My parents wanted me to visit on my lunch break since I had to work that day at a grocery store. I wasn't attending church regularly. Cupid hit hard as Ron and I visited during the picnic. I went back to work and told a coworker, "I just met the guy I'm gonna marry." Her response after I explained where I had been was, "You! Marry a minister?"

A few months later we had only had a few dates, one of which I paid my way. In all fairness, the Bible study we were on with one of the teens in the youth group had cancelled, so we would go to the movies together. We became engaged about nine months after I had met Ron. I had told him I was fine with being a minister's wife, just not a missionary. It's funny how sometimes we eat our words. We were engaged for six months and were married the Sunday before Christmas in 1987.

During those months, and after we were married, I used techniques to get Ron's attention that had worked for me as the "baby" of my family. These were not effective ways to develop a healthy relationship/marriage and usually created more stress, arguments, and dissension. As the youngest in my family, and entering my parent's world while they were older, I found it easy to pout, be stubborn, or ignore them in order to receive what I wanted. Many times one of us would be angry with the other. Even though we were able to talk out our issues, my previously useful behavior was not helpful in our relationship. Sometimes I found ways to get Ron's attention that were hurtful or incited a reaction. Other times I wanted him to pursue me and ask what was wrong. However, this was not a healthy or mature way to communicate. Ron was not my parent and I was not his child. We had to learn to share our feelings and anger safely and therefore respect each other as our partner.

This was especially important as we were doing ministry to teens, some who came from very dysfunctional homes and others who came from healthy homes. We were wanting to work together in ministry and we also realized that being a team in ministry meant we had to be healthy in our own relationship as well as when we had children in the future.

Ron

I came from a family that was dysfunctional. While my dad was not physically abusive, he was controlling and verbally abusive toward my mom and younger brother. He had abandoned his first set of children emotionally and physically, although he did send child support in the mail until they were eighteen years old. As the older son, I was more or less the "golden child" in both athletics and academics. While my dad had been physically abused by his parents, he did the best he could for me. I acknowledge that he was better than his parents, yet I have had to admit that his shortcomings were many. Due to this, I grew up with a father wound that took years to heal. My brother also grew up with this wound, but our differing birth orders and coping mechanisms have given us different tools in our lives, relationships, and own personal and spiritual growth.

When I came to our marriage table I brought behaviors that I saw in my father—whether I liked it or not. I behaved as I knew. I believed that women were there for men and could be used for our purposes. As a Christian, and one who was a youth minister, I had been given other models of Christian manhood by men in our churches. Some reinforced the "husband in charge" mentality, while others taught me a model of men respecting women and valuing their wives. While these two models were constantly before me, I found myself choosing what I was most "used" to being. This brought stress to our relationship, the Proverbs suggest that a "wise person listens to advice" (Prov 8:34; 13:10; 19:20). I didn't realize that the greatest advisor I might have would be the woman I was married to.

However I learned from Lori much about being in family. Many times birth order plays a large role in who we choose to marry. As the oldest child in a dysfunctional family, I had become a caretaker, the one who tried to keep my brother out of trouble, and the one who naturally tried to be in charge, in control, or organized. Those of us who play that role tend to become attracted to a spouse who played the opposite role. Lori was the youngest in her family. She was spontaneous, cared for, and more comfortable with relationships that did not demand structure. We did complement each other. While structure is important, it can also provide unnecessary stress on a relationship. While spontaneity is exciting, it can also bring its share of anxiety. Sometimes we like to be cared for, rescued, or guided. Other times this can be what angers us the most. Sometimes we feel good about caring for, rescuing, or guiding others. Other times it causes us to become frustrated with others and to feel unappreciated. Sometimes the partner we seek is the same one who "drives us crazy."

When I came to the table I found that what had been my survival skills and strengths, could be shared at the marriage table. Other times these strengths caused problems. I forgot that leaving my family of origin meant that we were beginning a new family, one that was not dysfunctional.

Our first few years of marriage were not only a time to find out who we were but to find out how wonderful the other person was. The hard tasks involved convincing myself that this family was different than the one I lived in for twenty years. To unlearn twenty years of history was difficult and could not be undone in our first year of marriage. Therefore, we set out on a journey to grow together, develop, and unlearn much of what we had been taught.

Whether what we had learned was healthy or unhealthy, the point was that we were a new family, and had to develop what worked for us. Some healthy behaviors enhanced our partnership. Some unhealthy behaviors were valuable teaching tools for our discussions and relationship. However, we were creating something new, and that was one of the exciting parts of our marriage. Even more, we had made a conscious decision to work out our issues and *both* do what was best for *our* relationship.

As a couple in ministry we also had normal stressors that joined us at the table. We moved after our first six months of marriage and transitioned from youth ministry in a large church to preaching ministry at a small-town congregation five hours distance from Lori's home. The tendency to over-function (a rewarding quality for ministers) had already been planted in my behavioral cortex. Much of our time as a couple involved setting healthy boundaries with our ministries so that our home, family, and marriage would be a safe space. In the beginning I would bring a large stack of books home to read at night. I had been used to working long hours and volunteering many weekends when I was single and tried to continue that after we were married. One night Lori asked me to put away the books and either pay attention to her when she talked to me or go to the office to read. I finally listened to Lori and admitted that this was "invading our sacred family space." It took a few times but I finally got her point (I am ashamed to admit I didn't get her point the first time she said it). I did not want to be a man who worked constantly and ignored my family, and I was already beginning to practice that pattern of behavior. I also know that deep down I didn't want to become a "workaholic" and needed to learn to leave work behind. I have come to see that ministry is one of those careers that will stay with you constantly both physically and mentally.

Making a clear break with work is important to one's family and their own health. It was important to remember that *we* were working for *us*, not *I* working for *me*.

> Frequently in the Christian subculture we espouse an ideal of selfless marriage. This is well-intentioned in that it seeks to place value on the importance of sacrifice and giving to the other, yet in so doing, we can unintentionally negate an essential component of relational intimacy. We argue here that when the Me, the individual identity, is not effectively regarded, the capacity to serve the Us becomes undermined . . . Selflessness or valuing of the other as more important than yourself must be preceded by a knowledge of the other's individuality and their knowledge of yours . . . This means that at the core of Us is a mutual understanding of both persons.[6]

6. Sells and Yarhouse, *Counseling Couples*, 52–55.

By listening to each other, I was learning not only to sacrifice for the relationship, but that Lori was sacrificing as well. While what worked well for *me* as a single man did not work well for *us*, I was realizing that I was benefitting in this relationship as well. As we set boundaries with ourselves, we also communicated to the congregation we served that we had set days off, and that I could not be someone who worked constantly. People responded by respecting our privacy, encouraging that we spend our days off together, and that others could pray until I was able to get to them. We communicated that as a minister I was not indispensable and that people would survive without my immediate attention. People knew that we would sit together in church, worship as a family, and try to do a ministry we could do as a team.

These boundaries helped us create our own safe space as a couple, and later for our children who would join our safe place in the future. However, I will admit that our first years of marriage were difficult as we were both trying to find our role on the team.

Conclusion

In Genesis God created the male and female relationship as a way of complementing each other so that they could live well. Men and women leave their families and unite to each other, merging and forming a new family. Each family is unique and distinct from their families of origin. This is because the couple forms a new team, embracing the best and worst of each person and their families. As a new team they learn to support each other by building on each one's best qualities and helping to heal their worst.

As humans who leave our families, we carry assumptions, behaviors, and attitudes from our families of origin. What may have worked in that family may be a driving force in our choices of a spouse or in how we survived. Yet, in forming a new family we spend time learning what is healthy and what is valuable to this new partnership. What may attract us to our partner or future partner, may also be something that causes anxiety, stress, or frustration in our relationship. The same is true of our partner.

Complementing each other is not always an easy task. To complete another person and help them to become a "whole" and "healthy" or "balanced" individual is a blessing, yet other times it causes frustration on either spouse. A healthy relationship is not built on one person fulfilling the same role, it requires spontaneity, adaptation, change, and stability. We are many times attracted to one who represents what we don't have, yet this is an opportunity to become someone different who reflects the harmony of this new relationship. We both have the opportunity to change and become more flexible in this relationship.

Sells and Yarhouse indicate, "There are two conflicting realities in regard to our culture's attitude toward marriage. The first is that marriage is seen as a passé institution that restricts individual happiness. The second is that first-time married couples report the highest degree of personal happiness compared with single, cohabitating or divorced adults."[7] We acknowledge that our parents began our maturing process and relationships further facilitates that growth. We have an opportunity to not only develop a healthy relationship in our own marriages, but we have the obligation to witness a healthy marriage/relationship for our children, friends, and those close to us. Marriage can be viewed as a dynamic relationship which is attractive, healing, and intimate. Marriage is not the end of the journey but a continuation of our development. It is not an institution but a relationship.

Complementing each other is God's tool to further define us, develop us, and mature us. Often males joke that when a guy marries, "It's all over." It is humorously described as the end of their freedom, life, and future. The photos taken before our wedding have pictures of Ron trying to escape with the groomsmen holding him back. While the wedding was something we were both excited to be a part of, it is still a tradition that continues even today. Women are groomed to be prepared for weddings, while males are expected to avoid them—and finally give in at the end. However, God designed marriage as a place for males and females to become better humans.

7. Ibid., 16.

In God's mind our differences are designed to be complementary, not to cause conflicts. This principle is illustrated by the Christian church, described in 1 Corinthians 12 as being similar to the human body—composed of ears, eyes, legs, feet, hands, arms, and so forth. Each member of the church is seen as an important part of the body. When everyone works in unity, each part enhances the others and together they serve the purposes of God. Similarly, in the institution of marriage, God intends for husbands and wives to bring their unique characteristics together to form one team that will work together under God's direction to accomplish his eternal purposes.[8]

What a powerful testimony that two people complement each other physically, emotionally, and spiritually. Marriage is an opportunity for these two people to leave their families, find the best in them and add it to their marriage table, witnessing their lives continue to transform.

This is why married couples can reflect the *we* image of God.

---

8. Chapman, *Four Seasons of Marriage*, location 1928.

Discussion Questions

1. Individually list what behaviors or skills you learned from your family of origin. Which can help your relationship? Which might not be helpful?

2. Share your findings with your partner. What skills do you have in common? What are unique to you? How can you combine these to help your relationship? What could be damaging?

3

Table for Two

Submit to each other ... (Eph 5:21)

Lori

WE ALL PRESENT DIFFERENT abilities to a marriage. I mentioned earlier about some of the difficulties I brought by being the "baby" of the family. Looking back, some strengths that I carried were being able to have discernment concerning people and choices that came our way. I have reminded Ron that discernment is a gift of the Holy Spirit. I still feel that God has sharpened this strength within me and has helped Ron develop this gift as we became church planters and worked in domestic and sexual violence. This has been our strength as we both decided to be trained in helping those in abuse. I was able to sense abusive individuals, and Ron would listen to me and support my calling for this gift.

When I met Ron he had a dog named "Puppy." She was a black Lab but didn't care for me. She loved the kids in the youth group, and they enjoyed having her around. However, for some reason she must have sensed that one of us was going to be the female of the house. While I was willing to resolve our differences, she would growl at me when I came over. Ron would tell me that he knew he would have to make a choice and it would be me.

When Ron went to summer camp with the youth group I would stop by his house to check on Puppy and make sure everything was secure. Unfortunately Puppy would break her chain and run to Kentucky Fried Chicken, which was one block away from his home. She would rummage through the trash and eat her fill then return, and she stunk! I had finally had enough chasing and her smelling like chicken trash. One day when I went by the house she was gone but I knew where to find her. She was in the trash at KFC. She tried to run from me but her chain was dragging behind and caught on the trash container. I drove home holding her chain outside the window and made her walk alongside the car. That day I called our local trading post on the radio, and Puppy found a good home. When Ron returned and asked where she was I told him the story. He wasn't too upset and said, well it was going to happen sometime. Ron was never afraid to support me in my decisions, and this one definitely needed to be made. Since then there have been many decisions that we have been able to talk out and work through together. As Gary Chapman wrote in his book *The Four Seasons of Marriage*, "In a marriage nothing is more fundamental than talking and listening. This simple transaction is the vehicle that allows couples to process life together as teammates. Open communication is the lifeblood that keeps a marriage in the spring and summer seasons. Conversely, failure to communicate is what brings on fall and winter."[1] We have always been able to talk and work our issues out together.

I always appreciate Ron's listening to me when he would be frustrated with our "youth group kids." Growing up in church gave me a little insight on having patience with those who struggled with their faith, choices, and walk with God. I struggled with church attendance and faith when I went through that period of my life. I also understood finding my own path and having my

---

1. Chapman, *Four Seasons of Marriage*, location 1521.

own faith. I am thankful to have a husband who encouraged me to question and find this path, where God leads me.

Ron

I barely remember the first time I met Lori. I was working a summer job, during college, at the Missouri State Fair with the Missouri Department of Conservation. We took care of a wildlife exhibit and managed the department's fair buildings throughout the state. At the State Fair we would let females bottle-feed the baby fawns we had for the summer. Usually we reserved this for the State Fair Queen contestants (we were three single guys that were twenty years old) or little kids. One day Lori and her friend were visiting. One of the guys was trying to flirt with her friend, and I remember having both her and Lori help us with the animals. Lori shared this with me a couple years after we were married. I didn't know it was her, but evidently I was flirting with her and she thought I was creepy.

Years later I met her at a church picnic. I had just moved to Chillicothe, Missouri to be the new youth minister, and the congregation had a potluck picnic to welcome me. We sat across the table and visited. I didn't think much of it afterward, but as time progressed we visited more and more. She was attending junior college near our town and worked at a grocery store. She helped me with the youth group girls and went with me on some of the Bible studies. I also saw how good she was with kids. She was one of the teachers I would have with our summer Vacation Bible School program (we would have upwards of two hundred children attend) and the younger girls seemed to like and respect her. She would come to church with her parents and we always talked.

We went out a couple times and would talk for hours. We both felt comfortable sharing things and talking with each other. The night before we became engaged I was faced with the difficult decision of sending a female intern home for unethical conduct. She and one of the youth group girls asked Lori to come advocate for her with me. They came to my house and I explained what had happened. They asked me to reconsider and said, "Lori can you talk to Ron?" She responded, "He's right—you can't do that. You need to go back home." I realized that she carried a lot of wisdom that I loved and respected. She stayed for dinner and we had a good evening.

The next night she invited me over to her home, since Van Halen had a concert shown on the television, something I did not own. That night we got engaged, and my life has been wonderful ever since. I asked her how she felt about being a minister's wife, and she said, "Fine, but I won't be a missionary . . ." We agreed and I respected her view. The funny thing about that statement is that within one year she went from being a college student working at a grocery store, to a youth minister, and then six months later, to a preacher's wife in South Missouri. When we resigned from preaching in Oregon to go plant a church in downtown Portland, a woman came to Lori, hugged her, and said, "So you are technically becoming a missionary." Lori laughed and agreed, and shared that she was excited to do this. From my perspective ministry and church planting have been the best thing for her; she reflects that same wisdom, patience, and love that I remember when she taught kids classes back in Missouri.

It has been many years, but time has helped both of us to draw closer to each other as well as God's will. If Jesus is Lord, he not only reconciles people to God and himself, but toward each other. We have both stated that our first love is Jesus, but if he is love, then we can't help but draw closer in love for each other. If we are commanded to love our neighbor, then why not our best friend and partner?

Two Becoming One

The Apostle Paul was not married while on the mission field. It seems likely that he had been married while a rabbi since he held a seat on the council and would have followed the typical Jewish customs expected of Pharisees, teachers, and Jewish leaders. However, when he wrote Ephesians 5, one of the most beautiful teachings concerning marriage, parenting, and household codes, he offered sound advice for families.

The letter to the Ephesians was written to a church existing in one of the largest cities in the Roman world. The city was considered a beautiful metropolis that boasted the temple of Artemis/Diana, which was considered one of the Seven Wonders of the World. In Paul's day the Ephesians worshipped Artemis, who was the huntress and the goddess of war, fertility, and the family. Ephesus boasted in the fact that it was the chosen capital of Asia and the protector of the goddess' home. In addition to this, Artemis was understood to be present at weddings and a partner in childbirth. Artemis was worshipped as the great mother and head of this city.[2]

In the Apostle Paul's letter to the Ephesians, he found a way to connect with the early Christians. First, Jesus was called "head" five times in the letter, instead of Artemis. Jesus also presided in marriage by uniting male and female, as the Ephesians believed that Artemis did. Finally, Jesus was lord of the home, family, and domestic relationships. Paul compared Jesus, as head, to a goddess.

Husbands and Wives under a Head

Submit to one another out of reverence for Christ (Eph 5:21)

The Apostle called the Christians to *mutual submission*. Years ago we were watching the reality show *Dancing with the Stars*. Christian actress Candace Cameron was one of the contestants and a common question she was repeatedly asked was, "How will you be able to dance with a male partner and still maintain submission to your husband?" It seemed like a criticism of Cameron, as if she could not control herself. It was also a criticism of her dance partner, Mark Ballas, and his intentions toward her as a professional instructor. There was no mention of "mutual submission" or even that the word submission strongly suggests "respect." The emphasis seemed to be on the "wife's submission" rather than the understanding that in a marriage both people submit/respect each other. Each decision is a

---

2. Clark, *Freeing the Oppressed*, 73–75.

team decision, a partnership, and a complement. Even more, during the show the husband was vocally portrayed as stating, "I support my wife's decision to do this and know that we trust each other." This important statement seemed to be minimized in the story. Paul called the early Christians to a radical marriage, one where *both* submitted to and respected each other.

How did husbands and wives submit to each other?

> Wives, submit yourselves to your own husbands as you do to the Lord. For the husband is head of the wife as Christ is head of the church, his body, of which he is the Savior. As the church submits to Christ, so wives submit to their husbands in everything. Husbands, love your wives, just like Christ loved the church and gave himself up for her to make her holy, cleansing her by the washing with water through the word, and to present her to himself as a radiant church, without stain or wrinkle or any other blemish; holy and blameless. Husbands must also love their wives as their own bodies. He who loves his wife loves himself. No one ever hated their own body, but feeds and cares for it, like Christ does the church—since we are members of his body. "For this reason a man will leave father and mother and is united to his wife, and the two will become one flesh." This is a mystery—but I am talking about Christ and the church. Each one of you also must love his wife as he loves himself, and the wife must respect her husband. (Eph 5:22—33)

Paul wrote this section to husbands and wives who worshipped together and sought to be transformed by Jesus. They had come to their marriage tables with their own family of origin behaviors. *Greek and Roman males tended to believe that women were weak, vulnerable, chaotic (sometimes evil), and irrational.* Therefore women were confined to the home and domestic duties while males were expected to be public, powerful, and aggressive. These were well-defined roles that were enforced by cultural etiquette and sometimes Roman law.[3] Males and females who violated these gender roles were dishonored and considered shameful to their

---

3. Clark, *Am I Sleeping*, 33–34.

families. Males who did not act like cultural males were labeled feminine (slaves, children, male prostitutes, and rape victims). Females who did not act like cultural females were oppressed and many times imprisoned or punished, except prostitutes and courtesans (who were allowed to roam in public with males). Respectable and honorable women were expected to occupy the female spaces in society, while honorable males occupied the public and honorable spaces in the city. Those who crossed these boundaries, whether by their vocation or by their own choosing, were considered shameful or inappropriate. In the church, males and females brought these "family values" to their marriage tables.

In addition to this, *males and females lived by culturally appropriate behaviors*. Males were allowed to have multiple sexual encounters, including same-sex encounters (as long as they played the "man" in the relationship). They were also expected to control their wives and children, and provide financially for their family. Females were expected to be sexually pure until marriage and faithful to their husbands, even if the husband was not faithful to them. They also were expected to manage their household, slaves, and children.

While Jewish families tended to be less like the Greeks, the Greek and Roman culture provided the more dominant cultural view in the churches where Paul developed congregations. When the males and females read Ephesians, they were men and women who had brought behaviors, beliefs, attitudes, and gender roles from their families of origin. Yet, notice what Paul wrote to these men and women.

First, *Jesus, not Artemis was the head of the community*. While some might view this as a direct affront to Artemis, it is also a comparison. Jesus not only ruled over all, he provided what Artemis provided. Artemis was thought to be the great mother who nurtured her community. Paul also suggested that Jesus nurtured his community by uniting all creation (Eph 1:10), by filling (nurturing) his body/people (1:23; 5:29), and maturing them/it through *agape* love (4:15). Of the Greek words for love, some meant sexual passion, others friendship, while the word *agape* indicated a deep and faithful love for an individual or those in a group. *Agape* is the self-sacrificing and unselfish giving that is shown through Jesus and his faithfulness as an all-powerful and loving God. *Agape* love is shown when individuals practice a love for others as part of a greater good, which in turn draws them closer to God. For the Apostle Paul, Jesus as head, was similar to Artemis the great head, mother, and uniting element of Ephesus and all Asia. While head can suggest authority, influence, source, or guidance; Jesus modeled service, *agape* love, nurturing and encouragement as head of his people.

Second, *as Artemis presided at weddings and united the couples, so Jesus united, presided, and made the marriage holy (sanctified) between the Christian men and women.* Christ saves, cleanses, loves sacrificially, and unites couples as well as the people of God. Again, Jesus is the head, much like Artemis, of the Ephesian/Asian people. Yet he, as a male, offered qualities that were viewed in Roman culture as being feminine. Today males are equally called to practice a family love that is countercultural and one that reflects Jesus, the head of the church.

Since Jesus was compared to a female goddess, in this letter, there are strong implications to couples in their marriage. *One implication is that marriage is truly a partnership.* As mentioned earlier, this partnership involves couples who complement each other and form a team, new family, and cleave as a couple. This is shown through Paul's encouragement for "mutual submission." When we practice mutual submission *we submit* rather than *she submits.* While there is much theological discussion concerning how Christian women submit to their husbands, we need to practice *mutual submission* (Eph 5:21). Women submit by respecting their husbands. Husbands submit to their wives by loving them, encouraging them to be the best they can be, and by nurturing and cherishing them. It is interesting that Paul offered more advice to men concerning their submission than to women, slaves, and children.

Even today males are called to nurture their wives. A similar term is used for fathers as well in Eph 6:1–4. In ancient cultures, slaves were hired to discipline and care for young boys, called *pedagogues.* They could be harsh or gentle, but most Roman males developed strong relationships with these babysitters. However, *pedagogue* is the word Paul used in this passage for father's instructing their children. For the Apostle, early Christian fathers were called to raise, teach, and work with their own children, rather than hire out a full-time attendant. This would have been viewed as women's or slave's work. Yet Paul called Christian fathers to be countercultural.

While there has also been much theological discussion concerning modern masculinity, being a real man, and the role of Christian males as "heads" of their families—the Apostle Paul did not hesitate to suggest that we husbands model a "headship" that nurtures, cherishes, and loves our wives. Even more, the majority of the text was written to males, suggesting that men have the greater responsibility and call for cultural change. Like Artemis, Jesus cared for his church. Like Artemis, Jesus sacrificed for his followers. Like Artemis, Jesus warmed and nurtured his followers. Today, males are not encouraged to nurture relationships, however Jesus left that model for us to follow.

Next, *if both husbands and wives submit to each other, a high level of respect will exist in marriages.* Couples who are married longer and have healthy relationships tend to practice positive comments and have a peaceful environment in their relationship.[4] Often, young couples spend much energy and time trying to maintain their individual identities and become critical, negative, and hurtful in their communication. Those who have been married for many years have learned that marriage is a team, and teammates succeed when they support each other. For the Apostle Paul, marriage is a relationship of mutual respect where both honor each other. The issue is not "who submits to whom?" but "how do we respect, support, and submit to each other?" In a culture where males are many times discouraged from being attentive and caring to females, Christianity offers another way, a new form of masculinity, and a unique relationship based on mutual support, love, respect, and submission.

Finally, *the best gift we could give our children is to have a strong and healthy marriage.* While we had not had children for

---

4. Gottman and Silver, *Seven Principles*, 5, 17.

our first five years of marriage, we worked with youth and witnessed firsthand the pain many felt living in a home where their parents (or stepparents) raised the level of anxiety through their destructive or unhealthy lifestyles. Children never expected their parents to be perfect, just loving. The love that we had for each other cannot help but spill over to our children, and others who come into our families. Even more, we knew the research and reality that children living in a spiritually focused home and active in a faith community tended to be emotionally and relationally healthy. Somehow living in a home with love, mercy, and support, as well as being in community that values those qualities, can drastically affect the growth and maturity of children. In our first few years of marriage we didn't own many possessions, but we knew what we wanted to do and how we wanted to love each other as we prepared for whatever future God had for us.

Conclusion

The Apostle Paul wrote that marriage was a reflection of the relationship between God/Jesus and the community of God. As the goddess Artemis, in Asia, was single and presided over marriage and childbirth, so the single Savior Jesus, presided over Christian marriage. When God unites a man and woman, they have an opportunity to form a new family and reflect the love and peace that is necessary in a relationship. Husband and wife help complement each other so that they can continue to grow and develop as humans reflecting God's glory. This happens when couples resist their cultural and family of origin influences to oppress or exploit each other. This exists when couples decide to build each other up and bless one another. When both express a love that nurtures and surrounds each of them, then spiritual, emotional, and physical growth becomes possible.

Marriage was always meant to be a relationship to be enhanced rather than an institution to be preserved!

Discussion Questions

1. What is "mutual submission"?
2. How are *respect* and *submission* related?
3. Discuss with your spouse/partner ways that each of you submit to or respect each other?

4

Sharing at a Table for Two

Wisdom is found in those who take advice ... (Prov 13:10)

HERMAN AND RUTH FRANKLE are a wonderful couple whom we met many years ago. Herman was a pediatrician who worked for the Center for Disease Control and taught at one of the prominent medical universities in Portland. Herman came to one of our domestic violence trainings to learn and partner in our work. After the training he shared, "When I came today I taught and believed strongly that the greatest event that damages children was divorce. Now, I realize that it is spousal abuse that is the greatest traumatic event for children."

From that time forward Dr. Frankle worked to develop a website for premarriage counseling that would guide individuals through questions, examples, and writing in order to observe the level of compatibility and offer information for the counselor to help and equip the couple to enhance their marriage from the beginning. Herman's key ingredient for the relationship was, "be kind to one another."

SHARING AT A TABLE FOR TWO

Kindness and Respect in Marriage

It sounds simple but it is very true. In our first few years of marriage we acted as immature adults. Young adults somehow have learned that being critical, snarky, using harsh teasing, and putting one another down represents a "normal" marriage. Maybe it's the many television sitcoms where husbands and wives take personal "digs" at each other. Maybe it's how we observe our parents interact if they may have had a miserable marriage. Maybe it's that men believe they can only criticize and point out faults to help one another become better? Maybe it's because women become overwhelmed and feel comfortable responding by cutting down their husbands. Whatever the explanation, negativity wounds one another and builds distrust. People who are hurt many times hurt others. It becomes a vicious cycle that may end with two people who are in love wounding each other so much that they create a chasm in their relationship.

Sells and Yarhouse suggest that it is not typically the fire that causes damage, but the smoke. "Marriages are not destroyed by events such as acts of infidelity, neglect or disrespect; marriages are destroyed by the pain produced by these events, and the disregard for the pain that husbands and wives carry. It's not the fire that kills, it's the smoke."[1] Smoke lingers, smoke penetrates and stains, smoke chokes, and smoke blinds. While putting out a fire can happen quickly the damage to a home is usually caused by smoke and water. Couples who aren't "kind to each other" can damage their relationship. Instead of watching each other's back, they blame the other for the arson.[2] This type of damage can linger for years and leave wounds and scars which will lead to mistrust and even disrespect. Sells and Yarhouse indicate that this is a cycle of self-defense and injury that will become a pattern and habit of negativity.[3] Couples must support each other in addressing conflict, even though they may have differing skills in handling this conflict. "The manner of

---

1. Sells and Yarhouse, *Counseling Couples*, 84.
2. Ibid.
3. Ibid., 81.

dealing with conflict for one spouse—that person's standard for conflict resolution—is not the same as that of the other."[4] This is why each can complement the other and work as a team to resolve an issue, rather than fighting each other.

Paul's advice to the Ephesian church was to nurture, respect, cherish, love, and honor each other. Mutual submission is not possible if mutual kindness and love (*agape*) do not exist. It is easier to nurture and respect a partner who builds us up, loves us, and treats us kindly. This is a "gracious cycle" that builds, develops, and produces mercy, forgiveness, and *agape*/love in a relationship. Paul lived in a time when males "had" women, and where women resented their husbands. Paul wrote that the growth of the Christian family would happen when both spouses treated each other kindly and respectfully. This is the idea of *mutual submission*, harmony, and unity.

Research on families that have been happily married for many years indicates that kindness and respect are key qualities of how the couple communicates.[5] One reason is that the couples realize that a team does not thrive when it is divided. Couples are a team and complementing each other requires support, respect, and being accepted and valued by the other member. They also have developed a pattern of respect and love for each other, manifested by positive and encouraging comments toward each other. Gottman and Silver call this "attunement" which means that the couple understand each other at a deeper level.[6] They understand how the other person actually "feels."

Agape Love Is Spiritual Maturity

Another reason for these qualities is that couples who become closer to each other do so because their love is based on mutuality. The Christian way suggests that *agape*/love is the greatest behavior that we can practice. While love has many definitions, Jesus taught

4. Bragg and Bragg, *Marriage on the Mend*, location 1519.
5. Sells and Yarhouse, *Counseling Couples*, 107–11; Gottman and Silver, *Seven Principles*, 5, 17.
6. Ibid., 83–84.

his disciples that the Greek word *agape* is the ultimate form of love. This form of love in the Bible is referred to as mature, complete, and sacrificial (Matt 5:44–48; 1 Cor 13:11; Eph 4:11–16). Spiritual maturity develops as one practices *agape*/love for Jesus, others, and ourselves. This is especially true in a marriage where both individuals understand that, as a team, they mature when *agape*/love is present. Often we hear that all people/relationships are imperfect, unhealthy, or dysfunctional. However, in planting a church named "Agape" we have come to realize that *agape* is a form of love that one has to choose. It requires a safe and affirming environment. As leaders there have been times we have had to confront bad behavior, but it was necessary to provide our community peace, safety, and respect for others. *Agape* is a love that expresses spiritual and emotional maturity as it transforms us and those we love. The way of *agape* leads to transformation and maturity.

Those who conduct research with human development from a spiritual background offer us an interesting challenge concerning maturity and communal relationships manifested by love. Humans are born as helpless babies but grow and mature in a loving and accepting community. As the community pours love into this new human, they not only grow but also learn to give back.[7] Maturity begins to happen when the individual reciprocates (gives back) to their community and the cycle continues. Humans develop in this complex web of relationships yet they are expected to mature by giving back and loving others.

While people are imperfect they can be mature, healthy, and functional. Relationships are designed to help individuals mature, develop, and grow in a healthy and safe manner. Dysfunctional, unhealthy, and immature people and relationships are destructive to not only the individuals in marriage, but their family and friends around them. We cannot accept excuses allowing couples to believe that relationships are stagnant and continue to settle for unhealthy relationships—our children need better models. They need to see that marriages are healing and dynamic relationships that empower us to be the best we can be for God. Young people from

---

7. Balswick, King, and Reimer, *Reciprocating Self*, 48–49, 88.

dysfunctional homes need healthy role models from their community as well. God's covenant involves two entities serving, loving, and working together in relationship. This covenant relationship was meant to be a place where people's spirit and sacred nature thrived and grew stronger. Covenants in the ancient world had stipulations and responsibilities, but also promised peace, blessings, and safety. God's relationship with humans offers these blessings, but also calls us to respond and offer love, faithfulness, loyalty, and respect for our Lord. Marriage, likewise, is a covenant relationship which is meant to help men and women unite, grow closer together, mature, and practice love. *Marriage is not an institution that need to be preserved, but a relationship that needs to be enhanced*!

Kindness and Respect Lead to Intimacy

Sexual attraction between couples is normal. We believe that sexual intimacy is not only a gift that each individual can share with the other, but it is what makes marriage unique compared to other relationships. Trust, support, love, and respect allows each of us to think of and please our partner, which fosters sexual intimacy. When Paul indicated to the Corinthian Christians that they not deprive each other of sexual relations, he was referring to the males—some of who were sexually active outside of their marriages but neglected their wives (1 Cor 7:5).[8] Often our culturally approved outlets for sexuality such as pornography, the sex industry, and extramarital affairs create a dependence on "self-pleasure," which are not designed to serve, love, and please our partners. This is especially true as pornography has moved into the mainstream of cultural communities through the internet and other venues. As Struthers wrote, "Over the years the pervasiveness of pornography has rendered men less sexually responsive to real women ... Pornography has numbed the healthy sexuality of men who are active consumers of it."[9] Habitual use of pornography can cause individuals to focus more on the "unreal relationship" of pornography and neglect the "real flesh and

8. Clark, *Better Way*, 67–68.
9. Struthers, *Wired for Intimacy*, 38.

blood" relationship of their partner.[10] It also opens the door to unhealthy and unsafe behavior in the marriage. Likewise the offended party in the marriage feels unsafe, hurt, and emotionally distant because of this "affair." This is why Christians believe, as Jesus said, that pornography is adultery (Matt 5:27–28).

Sexual desire between couples is declining due to the presence of "unreal" sexuality so common in our culture. In our work with those deeply engaged in these behaviors we find that there is a hurting spouse at home, who longs to be loved rather than neglected. This also breaks down the partnership of marriage. Being friends and loving each other is common sense in a marriage and offers a supportive and energizing relationship to a marriage. However showing mature, spiritual, and sacrificial love for one another is not only countercultural but it is a quality that catalyzes a relationship to thrive. When couples complement each other with love, mercy, grace, forgiveness, respect, and honor, a marriage grows stronger. Even more those who witness this relationship as family, children, or friends are deeply affected and moved to practice this same kindness and love in their relationships. We always share with couples that the greatest gift you can offer your children is to love each other passionately.

Terrance Real, in his book *How Can I Get Through To You?* offered some startling information concerning healthy and unhealthy marriages. As a marriage therapist he suggested that one third or more of the couples he has counseled are "not happy" in their marriages. "Conservatively, we can estimate that at least one out of three, perhaps one out of two, of those couples left standing do not relish their lives together."[11] He also wrote that longevity in marriage did not always produce healthy and happy relationships.

> Of the thousands of statistics about marriage churned out by social research each year, the one I find most depressing is that in all couples, rich and poor, happy and unhappy, one of the most reliable predictors of marital

---

10. Gottman and Silver, *What Makes Love Last?*, 62.
11. Real, *How Can I Get*, 33.

dissatisfaction is simple longevity. The longer couples live together, the lower their reported contentment.[12]

Think about that quote for a moment. When Ron first read this he had to read it again. It was a comment that shocked him. Later he shared this with Lori, and she reminded him of the many couples we had worked with in churches who manifested a tremendous amount of anxiety, tension, and dysfunction. Even outside of the abuse work we had done with families, we realized that those perceived as "normal" were actually hiding destructive or dysfunctional behavior. We began to discuss the leaders' wives who confessed to us feelings of neglect, abuse, or shame because of how their husbands treated them. We thought about the years when members would come to us with concerns in how leadership couples were behaving. We thought about the widowed women who confessed that they had been in a marriage prison for decades. We remembered the countless young people who poured out their hearts concerning the dysfunction and immaturity displayed in their parents' marriages. Even more we remembered the couples we blatantly saw carry out dysfunctional behavior and share that "no one is perfect."

While we understand that research exists that suggests that couples who stay married are healthier and live longer, we know that there is more to the studies.[13] Gottman and Silver refer to emotionally intelligent marriages which practice love, compassion, and peace. In our work with dysfunction and abuse we also know that there are many couples who have learned to "co-exist" or act as "two ships passing in the night." They live parallel lives and distrust each other. There are couples that stay married because their church has consistently told them that divorce is a sin (rather than divorce is caused by dysfunction or sin). There are abuse victims who feel that they have no way out of the relationship and live in the same home as their abuser. We know ministers who stand in court with an abusive male to support him while pressuring the

---

12. Ibid., 38.
13. Gottman and Silver, *Seven Principles*, 5.

female to forgive, return, and stay married. Longevity only proves that people have been together many years. We must move past simply believing that "longevity equals healthy marriages," and discuss healthy, loving, and happy relationships. Counselors will admit that the health of a relationship is not based on its existence, but it's dynamic. We must as well.

As church planters we also witnessed this firsthand. Within our first few years as a new church we discovered (actually we believe that the Holy Spirit uncovered) serious issues with some of our couples, such as affairs, neglect, abuse, sexual addictions, or other deeply unhealthy patterns of behavior. These were couples who had been in church since childhood and had been married many years. We had heard that new churches attracted people who are hiding something or from something, and we came to realize how true this statement was. We don't want to ignore the many good and healthy young couples we embraced at Agape, but we also heard many of their family of origin stories as kids raised in a "Christian" home. We found ourselves wondering if this was the new normal. We have, since then, listened to many young ministry couples ask us, "Is it just us, or do we seem to be the only healthy couple's in our network of friends or church?" However, we firmly believe that God's plan for marriage in Jesus is a relationship that offers love, trust, respect, joy, honor, and sexual intimacy.

Terrence Real's comment provided an eye opening discussion for us that evening, and many nights since. We knew he was right, yet we had a hard time admitting it. Maybe it was the many years of watching couple's praised at a church for "longevity" in their marriages without a discussion of the emotional and sexual health of their relationships. Maybe it was the many couples we counseled where one was victimized yet had been told that forgiving and sticking it out was more preferable than a divorce. Maybe it was the many adult children who shared their frustration at seeing their parent(s) praised, knowing what went on behind closed doors. Maybe it was the feelings we stuffed inside when we were told not to be judgmental and move on, when we saw deep sadness in a marriage.

We're not suggesting that longevity in a marriage is bad, nor are we suggesting that all marriages must be dysfunctional. We are not suggesting that all marriages have to be perfect either, but we do have a model for marriage in the Bible. We are not indicating that couples can't forgive, or that grace and mercy are not important in a marriage. What we are suggesting is that happiness and intimacy in a marriage is God's design. Jesus did not draw together a man and woman to live in sexual frustration, bitterness, resentment, distrust, dysfunction, or fear. He drew them together to be a witness of God's covenant with us. How we treat each other is a reflection to all of how Jesus treats his people.

Becoming Healthier

What happens if we experience this type of dysfunction or unhealthy relationship in our marriages? First, *we are often asked to speak concerning domestic abuse and controlling or manipulative behaviors.* We consider this Intimate Partner Violence and understand that it is the result of a power imbalance where one person oppresses the other. IPV is dangerous, and those who oppress others are highly dysfunctional and need to repent of their behavior. This can only be done with intensive therapy, and couples who experience this must actively seek a professional counselor, therapist, or talk to a minister who works with community advocates. We have a book that will help you understand this issue.[14] However, those who are victimized in this relationship must be aware that the offender must repent and do the work to change, and that God does not expect individuals to stay married to an abusive individual. Marriage is not a relationship of enslavement, but love, support, and empowerment.

Second, *couples who struggle with a dysfunctional relationship have many options for help.* The couple must admit and agree that this is a problem/sin that cannot continue. Jesus is honored by healthy marriages and those who admit to having unhealthy

---

14. Clark, *Freeing the Oppressed*.

relationships must decide (together) to make changes. One person cannot change a marriage or the other partner, therefore couples must begin to reconcile and restore their own individual relationships with Jesus. Requesting help from our church community and those men and women who are spiritual mentors can help us restore our relationship with God. Praying with them, our friends, and our spouse will help to draw closer to God and each other. We need to be part of a faith community if we want our marriages to be stronger. Third, the Bible says that "In the midst of many counselors/advisors is great wisdom" (Prov 11:14; 15:22). Seeking counseling or therapy from a qualified individual and healthy couple is important. It doesn't matter whether the counselor is faith-based or not, we know that counselors deeply desire to help couples work out their issues and, if possible, strive for reconciliation. Often we hear people speak negatively of counseling, but going to someone who is skilled at working with couples or individuals is wise practice. It is hard work, but they will push us to address any hidden issues and work to restore our relationships. Fourth, there are many resources written for couples wishing to heal, reconcile, repent, or grow together to become a healthy family. Some of the resources quoted in this book are good places to begin, but your church leaders will also know of helpful resources. Finally, continuing to surround ourselves with healthy couples to mentor us and listen to us as we grow and reconcile with God and each other will provide continual support well into our older years. In addition to this it will also eventually place us in the role of mentoring and guiding others.

A team cannot flourish when they do not work together. When watching beach volleyball at the Summer Olympics it becomes clear that each team member must fulfill their role, and many times help their partner with theirs. The duo constantly encourage each other, compensate for each other's mistakes or misses, and protect each other's talents. Likewise couples cannot succeed unless they love, support, nurture, and care for each other.

Reflections from the Marriage Table

Ron

As I mentioned earlier, my father's role model was one who was more critical of my mom and his children, who did not perform as they were expected. I became the one who overachieved, and my controlling behavior was done as a way to survive and make sure the rest of the family functioned. I easily micromanaged issues, protected my mother and brother, and tried to receive praise from a father who would do little of that—regardless of my accomplishments. When I one day challenged my dad and he backed down, my behavior became a source of control and power that I unfortunately used since had I "stood up to the old man." Instead of celebrating freedom that our family now experienced, I became the new person in charge. While my resistance to his behavior was a driving force for my passion for social justice, my becoming a man in this way reinforced the stereotypical masculinity, power, and domination.

When I came to our new marriage table I had to unlearn much of my survival techniques. First, *criticism was not something that helped the family stay safe—it became an unwelcomed guest at our table*. Lori did not need to be criticized, made better, or protected. She was a wonderful person, and I married her because I loved her and wanted to spend my life with her. However, my behavior quickly became something designed to "make her better," even though she had no need to change.

Once I offered to teach Lori Hebrew and promised I would buy her whatever "outfit" she wanted. I wanted her to realize that she had the ability to do this and could learn anything. Unfortunately that was a mistake as it only ended (after lesson two) with frustration. What I didn't realize was that if she wanted to learn something, she would do it herself, or she would ask my help. She did not need her husband trying to save her and "make her better." It was a hard lesson to learn and involved many arguments, but it was a lesson we learned early as a couple.

Years later when our oldest son, Nathan, became a teen, the typical father son arguments and clashes began to happen. By now

Sharing at a Table for Two

I had regretted standing up to my dad since I had heard so many "take on the old man," stories told by males whose conflicts involved physical violence. Some were dads who felt the need to "defend the throne and show the young buck his place." Other stories came from young men who either "overthrew the king in his castle" or "took a beating and realized that their dad was still in charge." In most of these stories the conflict was inevitable and regardless of the outcome, a valuable lesson had to be learned. The family without an attempted coup d'état was not normal. As I shared this with Lori she asked me, "Why does it have to always be that way?" I thought for a minute, and she continued, "You are not like your dad. He was bad, and you not only love your son, you tell him that often. It's not normal for dads and sons to fight, and I know that is not the kind of man or father you want to be." There it was, plain and simple. I had the power to change my own family dynamics. Dykstra, Cole, and Capps wrote this well, "Fathers struggle to connect with their boys typically because their fathers struggled to communicate with them . . . Fathers can take cues from wives in how they treat their sons."[15] Even more the Bible teaches that "A wise man/person listens to advice" (Prov 8:34; 13:10; 19:20). How much more wiser can we be by listening to our partner.

A second problem from my past family was that *Lori did not need to be rescued or saved*. She had held a job for many years and worked for an income as a single woman. She was a member at our church and had a great relationship with her parents and many in her town. She did not need a man saving her or coming to her rescue. She also did not wish to be a "helpless maiden" seeking a knight in armor to make her world safe. She needed a man to love her as she loved me. She needed someone to treat her kindly and respect her, as she respected me. I had brought much of my survival skills to the marriage table out of fear and control. I controlled my environment because I was afraid to not only fail, but make my "dad displeased" with me and my family.

What Lori helped me learn was that I was in a new family. This family was unique, different, and safe. There was no need to

---

15. Dykstra, Cole, and Capps, *Losers*, 2–3.

criticize, no need to be afraid and no need to control or rescue others. We were a team. We could change our past and create a safe environment where our children felt respected, loved, and could fail with permission. We could have a marriage that was not bitter but encouraging. We could have a relationship that was both passionate and mutually respectful. We could have a family that offered peace and kindness, rather than resentfulness. It was a new way of viewing marriage, but one that merged both of our strengths and weaknesses.

Lori

For the first few years of our marriage it seemed "fun" to be rescued and "cared for" in our relationship. I was five years younger than Ron, had only briefly lived completely on my own (my first year of college), and had worked in town while attending college and lived with my parents. After a few years what seemed "romantic" became a point of contention for me. It was not fun for me to be "taken care of," and I tended to resent Ron's attempts to do so. At times I expected him to do so but then would put up a front by resisting him and resenting him trying to "do for me." Ron would admit that he tended to treat me with less respect when this would happen and it created tension in our relationship.

As time passed and I began to tell him how this made me feel, I also realized that I needed to learn to be myself and not only ask for help but also ask him not to help me when I chose to do things on my own. I never really acted helpless, I would simply expect him to take care of things for me. As I sensed his frustration, I also communicated mine. We were learning that being a team and living together meant that we not only helped each other but empowered the other to do things themselves.

Sometimes it helped for us to decide, when something was important, who would do what needed to be completed and how the other would help. It seemed that when we were intentionally tackling an issue together, clearly defining what each could contribute and how the other could be supported was helpful.

Sharing at a Table for Two

Through time we knew each other's strengths and could naturally work together since one of us would know how to support the other. This has been especially important in working with our children, youth groups, and people in our congregation and community. As a convert, Ron tended to be more frustrated with the kids who were brought up in a Christian home and didn't quite grasp how important their baptism was to be as they lived their lives as new Christians. I identified with the teens since I once had experiences that they were having (and knew that our children would be in this position as well). However, Ron was much more patient with adults who were struggling to live out their calling after conversion. This was also true when we worked with males or females. We both were understanding how we could provide better ministry as a couple by listening to the other and learning from each other. Those with a father wound many times tended to relate to me well, and those with a mother wound would respond better to Ron than me. Sometimes the women in abuse or prostitution needed a female's voice of encouragement and support, while other times they needed to hear from a man that men could be honorable and compassionate. We learned to work together with males or females because God had not only given us gifts but expanded their usefulness when we worked as a team.

When our children were born we found that they likewise had different perspectives and sometimes one of us could understand better what they might be feeling or experiencing. If they marry we know that this will be true with their wives as well. In turn, the longer we have been married the more similar we have become, probably because we have listened enough to each other and begun to see relationships and people from various perspectives. We have also learned to trust each other's calling and work as partners in ministry. We do not undermine each other because we know that this will not honor Jesus or his calling for us in ministry.

Conclusion

Everyone who knew Herman and Ruth Frankle commented on how wonderful they were. At the public school where our church met each Sunday, I would pass by a plaque donated in honor of Ruth. Teachers shared how she volunteered after retirement as a school teacher. They would tell me how Ruth's smile lit up a room and how Herman's enthusiasm was contagious. We are better people because we have known this couple. They truly lived out what they believed. Be kind to each other and the rest will follow.

Discussion Questions

1. What is the difference between marriage as an institution and marriage as a relationship?
2. What are some of the ways you and your partner can help your relationship mature?
3. Discuss this with each other.

5

Filling the Table

Enjoy life with your spouse, whom you love, all the days of this bogus life ... (Eccl 9:9)

AFTER FIVE YEARS OF marriage our family began to grow. Our first son, Nathan, was born in Memphis, TN while Ron was in graduate school. He was taking a full load of classes trying to finish quickly while Lori worked full time. Ron would rise at 4:00 am to work part time at UPS, attend classes three days per week, and would study while not in class. Lori had a regularly scheduled job but could take Nathan to day care until Ron was able to pick him up after class or work.

We lived in a small trailer in the middle of wealthy Germantown, Tennessee. We were caretakers on a woman's property that offered low monthly rent. It was extremely difficult to leave a full-time ministry position to enroll in school, find new jobs for both of us, change health insurance, find a church community, and make new friends. Lori worked full time at a retail job that she didn't care for. Ron attended school and applied for countless jobs and was rejected. Lori became pregnant and our insurance dropped us. We had to apply for government assistance. We had always provided for ourselves, and probably looked down our noses at those who took government aid, yet the county workers were supportive, affirming, and reminded us that this is why we paid taxes. It was not only a hard time, but one that tempted us to be afraid and quit. We would question ourselves and God at times but still knew this was the right thing to do.

Fortunately we had a great church community. Many people prayed for us and we developed strong friends in our group of young married couples at church and school. However, we felt a strong sense of peace and knew that God would provide. We would survive and knew that we were doing what God had called us to do. Through time Ron received full insurance benefits. Nathan was born, and our church family, school family, and work families celebrated with us. We often opened our small trailer home to our students, people from our church, the youth group, and friends. We didn't have many things but we were always able to share what we had with others. Those two years were important as they taught us that sometimes our spirits grow in the simplest of times. Even more, they are a reminder that God provides. Our table was always full.

Nathan came along at a busy time in our lives, but one we knew was temporary. While it seemed, at the time, like Nathan had come at an unplanned period of our lives, it was actually something God had planned and probably was the best time for him to be born. It seemed easy to pull his high chair up to our small table and involve him in our conversation. We would entertain people from church, graduate students, and other friends in our small trailer but the table became the place where we would talk for hours, even Nathan. As a baby he had a short attention span and we usually passed him around the group.

Through time we left school and returned to preaching at our previous congregation in Missouri. We bought a newer table and expanded our size. We were able to eat many meals at the table and engage our son in conversation. However, we noticed that as our friends had children, meals were different. The kids gobbled their food and ran outside or into another room to play while we visited. They returned to snack but left as quickly as they had come. We even expanded the meals into our yard by purchasing a picnic table and small 'breakfast table" for our back porch. It didn't matter which table we used. We would sit, eat, and talk for hours. Many times each table had its own conversation or group when people would visit.

When we moved to Oregon we were given a heavy oak table that was well-worn, sturdy, and difficult to move. It had been used by a family that no longer needed it and eventually divorced. Like our marriage, the table was a lesson from someone else's relationship. Over the years we learned from others what was healthy, what was not, and what would last. Bits and pieces of wisdom were gathered throughout our relationship, and we discussed and shared with each other the meanings that were important to us.

This new table not only welcomed our son Nathan but our next two sons, Hunter and Caleb. Hunter came ten years after Nathan, at a time when we were at a large church preaching and experiencing a stable ministry. Caleb came two and one half years after Hunter, as we were considering leaving to plant a new church. This new table withstood the tension from two more high chairs and welcomed the new boys. It was large and seated six, enough for our ever-expanding family. The table was well-worn, had many stories to tell, and yet was solid.

Our marriage table had changed. We no longer could sit just the two of us and talk for hours. We now had to engage three others into the conversations. Three different levels of communication had to exist at the same time. We instituted "ups" and "downs" during this time and included visitors when they ate with us. We would ask each one of us, "What was your up today?" and "What was your down today?" which gave us something to talk about each night. When the boys gobbled their food and left, we tried to talk as we did in the past, but the reality was—we were tired. We would do the dishes together and talk but many times those evenings were a blur. Our marriage table was used, but it was worn.

Filling the Table

Sometimes we ate on the couch and watched television. These originally were reserved for the occasional "Pizza Night," but it became easier after a hard day to make supper and eat in front of the television. Falling into "habits" sometimes may make things easier, but after time we began to realize that we needed to be intentional and return to our old friend, *the table*! This friend seemed to provide that structure and sharing that we would miss "on the couch."

Pessimist or Optimist

The writer of Ecclesiastes has often been viewed as a pessimist. Throughout the book he used the word "vanity" or "meaningless" thirty-one times in twelve chapters. The Hebrew word is similar to the word for "Abel," who was the son of Adam and Eve. Abel appears for a short moment in the Genesis account until he is murdered by his brother Cain. Abel, like his Hebrew name, dissipated quickly and left a fleeting mark in Bible history. A more modern word that could be used would be "bogus."

For some, the writer was understood as being overwhelmed with the emptiness of life and wrote that life is a vapor that will vanish quickly. This has led some to believe that the theme of the book is, "life is meaningless, so just enjoy what you have." It is thought to create a sense of sadness and sorrow for those who feel that life is negative, empty, or a passing vapor.

However, the writer extensively mentioned, in eight sections, that one's lot is to enjoy life. The writer suggested that since life is a vapor, we might as well celebrate and enjoy what we have.

> Go ahead and eat your food with happiness. Drink your wine joyfully because God favors what you do. Always wear white and anoint your head with oil. Enjoy life with your wife, whom you love, all the days of this bogus life, which God has given you under the sun—every bogus one of them. For this is your lot in life and in your hard labor under the sun. (Ecc 9:7—9)

Reflections from the Marriage Table

A godly life involves enjoying food, drink, clothes, our jobs, and our spouses whom we love. Notice the emphasis on the spouse, "whom you love . . ." Marriage is to be enjoyed, celebrated, and something that gets us through the overwhelming and depressing days of our lives. One who may be weak in their faith may many times become overcome by the disparity of life, but God offers us a new perspective—a chance to enjoy what we have been given, because they remind us that life is worth living. To enjoy our marriages and family relationships is not only a blessing from God, it is a joy that reflects our faithfulness and love toward God and each other.

First, *the writer suggested that our marriages are to be enjoyed, embraced, and celebrated.* As our table grew, our boys entered our "sacred time." We adjusted by including them in our discussions, taught them to cook with us, and invited them to help with preparations and cleaning up. Our dinner times were always something we celebrated together. No matter how bad the day would be, we knew that the table was a place to talk about our day and what good and bad things happened. Lori introduced the "What was your up today?" and "What was your down today?" When we had guests join us they were invited into the conversation, preparation of food, and stories. We often talk about how people always seemed to congregate in our kitchen and dining room rather than the living rooms. For some reason these smaller spaces were where people would come and visit with us.

The writer of Ecclesiastes *also suggested that our marriages needed to be enjoyed due to the futility of life.* Work, school, serving people, and current events can wreck our self-esteem or view of the future. A bad day can stay with us for a long time. However, eating, drinking, and enjoying our meal can help to resolve those days and cope with the next day. A person doesn't have to "drink" their problems away because they will still be there when they awaken. Yet, the dinner table can become a place where we develop confidence to face our problems and address them the next day. As parents these conversations gave us opportunities to intervene in something that the boys had difficulty addressing. We heard how our children were learning to compensate for an issue and heard their plans to solve a problem. We learned that they had a sense of humor (boys can laugh at more than just passing gas). We also found ways to parent together at the table and could later discuss what we needed to do. We often heard from our guests and their friends that their homes did not enjoy family meals as much. This is a sad commentary on many homes, marriages, and relationships but one that can be healed at the marriage table.

It is also important to have a safe place due to the high levels of anxiety and drama that families face. We live in a time when social media portrays individuals/families in a better light than they really are. Often people appear one way in social media but are overwhelmed with unhealthy issues at home. For some, this illusion takes tremendous amounts of emotional energy. Others realize that constructing a stable appearance might become too time consuming but will give them a sense of honor and respect. It is easy for families to focus on the appearance rather than the reality. It can also be easy to base our opinions of what is healthy by the assumptions of one's perceived success or the media posts of others.

The dinner table is authentic. People eat, talk, and unwind at a dinner table. We have found that when we gather to eat, and invite others to join us, people tend to comment on how relaxed they feel. God designed meals to do this. It is remarkable that the last memorable event Jesus had with his disciples involved a meal. For our family, no matter how bad the day had been, sharing our "ups" and "downs" was always something that brought a sense of peace. The table is an opportunity to be at peace and honest with those we love. It is a time to enjoy who and what God has given us. That is why we give thanks.

Finally, *we found that once again the table became a stable element in our marriage.* As with most couples, growing families, working full time, raising children, and trying to keep a clean house can be exhausting (especially if you have little children later in life). There are times when intimacy is a fleeting thought. There are times when eating at a restaurant without a play land is your best night out. There are times when the kids go down to bed and you follow ten minutes later. That's marriage. It doesn't mean anything is wrong. It just illustrates that marriage can be hard work. Survival is possible, but one that requires commitment from both individuals. Yet the meal/table can be a time/place where we slow down and regroup.

It's what we sometimes call the "grinding it out" time of a marriage.

It gets better.

As a couple who planted a new church in downtown Portland, we found that the table was also a place to share our dreams and how our ministries were doing. Our house had become our first meeting location for nine months, and we had many meals with our core group of people over those months. While the work was hard and both Lori and Ron were exhausted, somehow eating a meal was not only central to our family, it had become central to our faith that we were practicing daily with this new church. We had numerous staff, leadership, ministry, premarriage and marriage counseling, and home community meals around the table. Plans were made. Stories and successes were shared. Intimate thoughts and struggles were sometimes expressed. There were times when we worked in the community and inviting the team or committee for a meal or cookout followed by a meeting seemed like a good idea. They always ended with hugs, smiles, and new friendships.

The meal can be the best time to connect with each other. Everyone is usually awake, hungry, and ready to talk. While children will grow, intimacy with couples will rise, and our energy levels may return, eating a meal at the table will always be a priority. For us it was a stable time when we knew we would be there to visit. It didn't matter if there was a fight, or if two people were angry with each other, or if we hadn't been able to talk all day. Somehow saying, "Please pass this" or "This is good" or "What was you're up today?" are statements that can encourage us to talk to each other. The marriage table once again became the place where relationships were maintained, developed, and enhanced.

FILLING THE TABLE

Discussion Questions

1. How can "the table" become a stable element for a family struggling to survive?
2. What are some of the daily issues/struggles that couples (you?) may face as they try to grow and work together?
3. What can/do we enjoy about our marriages and relationships?

6

Stories and Ministry from the Table

God has called us to live in peace ... (1 Cor 7:15)

MINISTRY IS NOT ONLY hard on those leading in churches, it is hard on their families. We have heard many stories concerning ministers, their spouses, and children of ministry couples. Some have been disturbing while others have been very affirming. As a whole, the typical story we hear from adult children of ministers is that their father was often absent. One former minister's wife, whom we respected deeply, shared with us that her husband was expected to minister to God, the church, and their family—in that order. She gave a strong warning to us as a young couple that we not be pulled into this pattern and to remember that the family is our greatest achievement for God. Too often her husband was too exhausted to help with the children, and while their children were spiritual as adults, they had suffered the price of their father being available to the whole church before he was available to them.

We had both decided early on that this would not be the case with our marriage and family. When we were first married our preacher's wife shared with us that because ministers were not well paid, Lori would need to work and both of us would have to work as a team to raise their children. Since then many women have shared some important stories with us that formed us as a couple in ministry.

While Jesus did call his apostles to leave their families and follow him, he promised to provide more in the "renewal of all things" or the "age to come" (Matt 19:27; Mark 10:30). Often those in ministry use Jesus' call to abandon "everything" as a way to support sacrificing their family to preach the Gospel and do ministry. While Jesus did teach this, before he ascended, the teaching of the early Christians challenged Christian parents to be involved in their families. Paul indicated that the apostles (including Peter) were accompanied by their wives (1 Cor 9:5). He also wrote that Christian leaders needed to be personally involved in raising their children. He did not use the common Greek word for "management" of a home (that was used by current Greek and Roman teachers) but intentionally chose the word for "involvement" as a style of leadership (1 Tim 3:4).[1] For Paul, a leader's ability to be involved with their family was a reflection on their ability to spiritually lead a community. In a culture that encouraged men to delegate child-rearing to women and slaves, Paul called them to be countercultural.

While balance has become a common term for families seeking to maintain peace, we suggest that *Shalom* be a better term. The Jewish concept of Shalom (peace) and Sabbath (rest) reflected an environment of justice, safety, holiness, rest, and peace. It was not the absence of conflict, but the presence of safety. Marriage authors Harville Hendrix and Helen Hunt label this the "imago" space, or the safe space between couples.[2] This safe space, where the Spirit dwells and the image of God thrives, provides couples and families the opportunity to foster trust, respect, love, and honor. When we enter that space we must maintain peace and safety.

Often we hear people discuss "balance" in a culture that increases demands for parents and children. This balance seems to be a difficult demand and may add more stress to an overburdened

1. Clark, "Family Management," 245–48.
2. Hendrix and Hunt, *New Way to Love*, 3–10.

family. However, peace/Shalom is possible even in a fast paced and hectic society. Ministry provides a difficult problem to families seeking to love Jesus, each other, and others while navigating an ever-changing society. We knew that ministry would not only be a blessing in our lives and for our families, but it could also be something that brought chaos. Our goal was to provide Shalom and Sabbath in the midst of a hectic and fast-paced culture adding stress, anxiety, and chaos to our relationships. However, we knew that God offered something better and a peace that could grow among us, creating an environment that would be safe, exciting, and sacred.

Intentionality

First, *we believed that our marriage and family had to be intentional.* If we had children, we would consider them a gift from God and understand that we had a responsibility to them, Jesus, and each other. Being intentional about our marriage involved more than deciding to never divorce. It meant we would not let anything, anyone, or any responsibility drive a wedge between our relationships. Being intentional about our family was more than deciding that our children would grow up to be active Christians. It meant that we would be available to them emotionally, physically, and spiritually. We understood that people will make choices, but we decided to be the people and family who would try to be who God called us to be, and would love each other unconditionally. We understood that relationship streets ran both ways, therefore we would do our part to contribute positively to our relationships. Marriage, love, relationships, and parenting did not "happen," they were active verbs requiring us to commit to their direction. This is what it means to be intentional.

Over the years we have not only counseled couples, but also worked with intimate partner violence and sexual assault victims and offenders, those experiencing adultery, dysfunctional families, and families with addictions. We have witnessed many leadership couples in ministry as well as those in our own churches in their relationships and behavior. Many have taught us healthy patterns for our own marriage and family. Unfortunately many more have shown us unhealthy behaviors. We believe that intentionality played a major role in the decisions couples and parents faced in their relationships. Intentionality happens when a spouse "thinks like a spouse," or a parent "thinks like a parent." "I am married—how would my spouse feel about this?" is an intentional question. "I am a parent—how would my children feel about this?" is also an intentional question. Once we enter into a covenant relationship, "I" becomes "we," and therefore "I" have to intentionally think about "us." Our choices no longer affect just me, but my spouse and family as well.

In a blended family, intentionality is extremely important. Former partners and stepchildren can intentionally or unintentionally create friction between the couple. Parenting and growing closer in a marriage are difficult but if the couple is intentional and aware of the struggles of blending families, they can perceive potential problems ahead of time and work together as a team. Communicating to stepchildren and those who are adopted that "we are committed to this relationship" will help them in their decisions as family leaders. Supporting the other parent or stepparent in working with the children is important to keep the family healthy. Even the "ex-spouse" has an opportunity to intentionally help the family provide safety in both households by doing what is best for the children and their parents.

Many of the problems couples face happen because *both* are not intentional in their relationship. Dysfunction can occur if only one person is intentional concerning the relationship, causing one to "over-function" to keep the marriage bond. This is not teamwork. The Bible teaches that God has not ordained relationships/covenants to be one sided. Both individuals in a covenant have obligations—covenants are broken when one partner mistreats the other. The nation of Judah was sent into exile (also referred to as a divorce) because they failed to keep their relational vows to God (Jer 3:8). The Lord became a witness to us that those who suffer in relationships have the right (and responsibility) to say "enough."

The offending party has the responsibility to make amends, repent, validate those they hurt, and change their behaviors to honor their relationship and partner.

When individuals/couples are intentional in their relationships, they make sacrifices and decisions that are best for their families. Some work to remove and stop practicing their addictive behaviors that brought stress, shame, or pain to those who love them. Others may choose to stop a habit that they know makes their spouse or children uncomfortable. Some ask what others in their family *need* (not just what they want) from them and try to provide what they can. Others may realize that behaviors learned in the family of origin create more distance in their families because they are different. Some provide space and support while those in the family grow to become who God calls them to be. Spouses and parents who are intentional in their family relationships see themselves as "we" rather than "me" and make choices based on this view.

This also applies to careers. We admit that due to the economic struggles of many families in America who are part of the dissipating middle class living in poverty, balancing work and family is difficult. Both parents often have to work jobs (sometimes more than one) in order to provide for their families. No longer should we believe that families work many hours because of the desire to live an extravagant lifestyle. After spending years working with homeless individuals, low-income families, and reading the research concerning poverty in America, we have to admit that both parents may have to work just to survive. Wages continue to be low, housing/rent continues to increase, and employers sometimes place unrealistic expectations on working parents/spouses. However, many times work, careers, and an inability or fear of telling a boss "no" can interfere with family time. For single parents trying to juggle visitation, child support payments, and being present, the struggle is even harder. Yet, being intentional allows us the opportunity to think about our families when making decisions about work, overtime, or extra time on our jobs. The old excuse, "I work hard so that you can have these nice things," means little when the children become adults. They do not always view this as a reality but an excuse. Parents have a greater influence on their children when they make sacrifices for their families. We have many times indicated to people that it is easier to start a new job than it is to begin a new family.

As a couple in ministry, this always became a struggle. There was always another person to visit, another book to read, and another hour to spend toward ministry, or another meeting to attend. There was always a conference, event, or mission trip to attend for a week. Intentionality reminded us that if one of us is gone, the other had to work and take care of the kids. Even more, it was an extended period of time that we would ask our spouse to be without intimacy until we returned. The Apostle Paul reminded the early Christian couples that being apart physically might be a spiritual time, but it put the other spouse at risk and should be done by consent from both individuals (1 Cor 7:5). Intentionality suggests that we ask what is best for those who stay behind and choose not to put them at risk. Even more it is an opportunity to show our families our love by what we give for them.

Additionally, we know that there are those whose professions require extensive deployment, travel, and separation from families. However we have always urged the families to work together and seek to do what is best for their family team and to keep their relationship strong. As the Apostle Paul wrote, "God has called us to peace," (1 Cor 7:16).

Presence

We also believed that we needed to be present for each other and our children. When we were first married this was difficult and as time passed it has become more difficult. With social media, individualized smartphones, game systems, and tablets it has become easy to disconnect from each other and spend most of our time online. It is easy to become more aware of what occurs globally than in our own living rooms. Even more, children and adults who extensively play electronics have a hard time stopping to eat, spend time talking, or doing chores. Time can quickly pass when we are online, therefore boundaries are needed for both parents and children.

While we have never felt that these electronic games or computers were bad, we recognize that they can withhold our attention and distract us from other things we may need to do. We often discuss how much more pleasant road trips can be when the kids can become occupied with their electronics while we visit in the front seat. We realize that time in the car is more pleasant than when we were children ("Are we there yet?"), and there are more things to keep their attention. We realize that children need time to unwind after school or on their holidays. While we acknowledge that "screen time" should be limited for children (and adults), we have always felt it was not harmful for our children to have these devices. Over the years, television, social media, game systems, music, and online systems have been blamed for societal ills; yet we believe that these are not the cause of all family issues.

If parents and spouses are intentional concerning their family relationships, they will also be present. Our families need us physically, emotionally, and spiritually. Often we hear from adults who struggled with father/parent wounds that their parents "weren't there for them." It is possible to be present in a room with each other and not "be present."

First, *we realized that our children needed us physically present*. Ron made the decision when we were married to never miss a birthday, special holiday, or celebration. Ministers can always find a conference, speaking engagement, or retreat in which to be gone. This was a sacrifice and sometimes it meant flying home late the night before one of these days, leaving the day after, or missing an entire speaking engagement. Planning travel around the birth of our sons in order to be home two months before and six months after seemed difficult at the time. In looking back we realized that it was a small sacrifice and one well worth it. We have always spent special days together and being present was more important than whether or not this was interesting, fun, or "the best use of our time." Those we love do not care *why* we are there—they care *that* we are there. They do not remember *what* we did, they remember *that* we did. We realized that our family appreciated the sacrifice, and would grow up to remember it, whether they immediately acknowledged it or not.

Many times children who are adopted experience "attachment syndrome" where, because they struggle to understand why they were abandoned by their biological parents, they project their anger and anxiety on the caregivers. This is difficult for parents to experience as they feel the brunt of the child's anger. Families sometimes adapt by avoiding the anger and distancing themselves from the child (this also can happen with stepchildren). The more they withdraw, the more the child feels abandoned and wonders if they can "drive away the parent." This also affects the couple's relationship as one parent typically tries to stay connected to the child while the other begins to work longer hours, stay away from the home, or focus more energy connecting to another child. While this is a painful time both parents must intentionally be present and show the children that relationships involve resolving anger, loving confrontation, loyalty, and presence. As the children mature they will remember that their parents "were there."

Second, *emotional presence is necessary for our families*. Children exist in a quick-paced world. They live in societies which offer various influences on their emotional, sexual, physical, and intellectual development. The home must be a safe place for children to enter, unwind, and be at peace. The Bible teaches us that God's kingdom/community should be a place of Sabbath/rest and Shalom/peace, which includes justice, safety, love, and support. This is what is known as sacred space or safe space. Children who live in a sacred/safe space will develop, mature, and grow to be who God created them to be. Likewise, children who live in environments where there is violence, fear, high anxiety, tension, yelling, negative noise, and threats to their safety develop a wide range of emotional, physical, and mental maladies. Children who live in safe/sacred spaces are able to thrive in an environment that supports and nurtures them.

As parents we knew that our boys needed safe places to grow. We knew that our relationship could help them develop and mature in a healthy manner.

> The stress children internalize from what occurs between their parents or stepparents often manifests in the classroom and the playground. For example, students who are caught in the middle of marital turmoil often have difficulty focusing on their classwork, and their progress in school wanes as a result. Inappropriate behavior, missing homework, and poor physical health are just a few of the external signs that there may be problems at home. Adult children obviously exhibit different signs than younger children do. What matters is for you to realize that regardless of their ages at the time of your crisis, separation, or divorce, their trust in you has been dramatically impacted. You must be willing to rise up, shelter them from further harm, and intentionally rebuild the trust of each child involved.[3]

Children face pressures from school, work, athletics, music and theater performances, friendships, and sometimes dating. While most of the time children's experiences in these environments are positive, there are those days when our children come to the table discouraged or frustrated. Parents have an opportunity to listen, support, and problem solve with them. Our boys needed to learn to self-soothe as babies as well as when they were teenagers. Many times teenagers experience diverse emotions during puberty, but the home is where they should be able to express themselves and learn to adapt.

Safe places are difficult to create. In a safe space, family members, like Job in the Bible, have the opportunity to speak their mind. Safe places allow for members to learn how to be honest, open, and safely confrontational. As parents, we would rather our children feel free to speak more openly to us than they might with their teachers or other adults in public. What might seem as disrespectful language toward parents may be a young person's

---

3. Bragg and Bragg, *Marriage on the Mend*, location 1384.

attempt to be honest. We would rather our kids learn how to speak directly and honestly in a respectful manner—however they will have to learn to do that from their parents. The home should be a place to make mistakes, learn how to communicate respectfully and honestly, and feel safe developing healthy skills for society. Emotionally we offer to listen and help them communicate outside our families respectfully. Many times children are not speaking to us disrespectfully because they are not sure how to say what they think. Emotionally safe families give permission to children to learn to communicate their feelings as well as listen to others.

Sacred spaces allow for sadness, sorrow, joy, pain, elation, and fun. Parents who struggle to express these emotions adequately themselves, pass this struggle to their children. Parents who live with high personal anxiety also transfer this to their children and can respond by attempting to control them, or fail to set healthy boundaries and "fuse" with their children.[4] However, parents who know how to live in peace and create safe spaces have children who naturally develop calm spirits. We had an older friend in our church who used to tell us, "Happy babies have happy parents. Calm babies have calm parents." She would remind us that our level of anxiety many times would affect our children's as well. It was important for us to continue to work together to offer a peaceful, happy, and safe environment for our boys.

Finally, *spiritual presence will live in our family's memories for many years after we are gone*. Over the years we have had parents tell us that they chose a church based on the youth group, or because their children liked the congregation. Other times parents would tell us that they decided to return to church because their kids were getting older. It seems that many times adults feel that church, spirituality, and the stories concerning Jesus are only for kids.[5] Unfortunately, when the children leave home, become frustrated with the youth group, or go through the "leaving church" phase of life the parents are left attending a church where they are

4. Sells and Yarhouse, *Counseling Couples*, 143; Gilbert, *Eight Concepts*, 11, 21; Richardson, *Creating a Healthier Church*, 80.

5. Bergler, *Juvenalization*, 10–12.

not as committed. The reality is that in the Bible the parents were to model, teach, and lead their children in the ways of God (Deut 6:6–10). A relationship with Jesus is taught, not caught. While our children's ministry, youth ministry, and youth leaders do an excellent job of teaching our children; the reality is that children learn best from their parents' example.

We have witnessed the struggle of young adults who are attempting to break from the negative spiritual influences of their parents. While many understand what Jesus wants from us, the pattern of behavior witnessed in their homes has a powerful impression on their lives, choices, and beliefs. While many know the good and bad that they observed in their parents, the reality is that their parents "modeled" behavior has made it difficult to break a dysfunctional cycle. Many will continue to struggle unless they break from their parents influence and accept the guidance and leadership of another father or mother figure in their lives. This is why marriage mentoring and discipleship are such important ministries in our churches.[6] Researchers at Biola University have also produced evidence that spiritual faculty members who mentor incoming freshman from nonreligious homes have a tremendous impact on their faith.[7] Upon graduation, these students had developed their faith to a level equal to or greater than their peers who came from religious homes. Christian leaders who mentor younger people clearly play an important role in faith development. Young people need to actively engage mature spiritual adults who can guide them to become mature followers of Christ.

On the other hand, we have experienced young adults whose parents were wonderful models of Jesus and spiritual maturity. Some had parents active in ministry or church leadership. There is a sense of stability that we find from many of these young men and women who learned from their parents to support the vision and goals of the kingdom of God. They possess a solid commitment to both growing spiritually and becoming leaders in their community.

---

6. Dunn and Sundane, *Shaping the Journey*, 18–19; Sell, *Transitions*, 27–32.
7. TenElshof and Furrow, "Role of Secure Attachment," 99–108.

While they all had differing levels of commitment or knowledge of the Bible, they tended to be respectful and open to learning.

We do feel compelled to write a note concerning children raised in Christian homes and their choices to follow or reject church when they become adults. Many parents have carried deep emotional grief and shame over their children's choice to leave church (or leave their church affiliation). When we worked in youth ministry we witnessed children who grew up in homes that did not practice Jesus' way of discipleship and who grew to become adults active in their church and later became leaders. We acknowledged that the home may not have been the place of faith and learning concerning Jesus, but the parents may have taught them valuable behaviors that were important in their lives. Some children lived in Christian homes and walked away from regular church attendances as adults. While they may have been good, morally honest, and hard-working adults, the parents felt that they had failed as Christian parents. Sometimes the church, other Christians, or leaders added to this shame by blaming the parents for their children's choices. We had children tell us that they respected their parents and the values they were taught, but at this time church was not for them. We also witnessed parents who were controlling as Christians, confrontational, and sometimes hypocritical, raise children who stayed in church and raised their families in a spiritual home. We learned as youth ministers that we could not help people if we judged them by the choices of others.

- We did not blame Jesus when people walked away from him. Even Judas!
- We did not blame church leaders when people practiced sin in church or left the community.
- Therefore, why should we blame parents for raising their children in a spiritual community that believed in "free will" as a blessing from God?

Biblical texts such as Prov 22:6 have been misused to assume that children will automatically follow the way of their parents.[8] As parents we can only teach, disciple, and impress our children of the values that we are willing to practice in our lives. Regardless of what our children choose, we want them to respect, value, and honor what we have practiced as adults who follow Jesus. When our children become adults they will feel safe, at peace, and open with us when they come to visit and bring their children to us. Whether or not they choose to practice our belief system, they will be able to witness that "our parents live what they believe."

Individuation

As mentioned earlier, differentiation is the ability to develop healthy relationships and set boundaries with others. *We believed that we needed to develop healthy individuals who could also thrive and develop in relationships.* Healthy individuals can be alone (solitude) and yet be in a relationship. Healthy couples can have time together where both feel safe and yet have time away from each other while trusting and believing in the other. This is true both for couples and children in a family.

In a family system there exists two groups. *The first group is the couple/parents.* The level of intimacy that exists with this couple is vastly different from the relationship with the children. Couples are sexually intimate with each other, guard their time together, build each other up, serve and nurture each other, and have adult and healthy conversations. Their relationship continues long after the children leave home. They are able to build a strong relationship that works as one. They also are trusting of each other and encourage each other to have alone time, time with other friends, time at work, and relationships with the children. Couples do not feel threatened by the other's relationships when both love each other and are intentional and present. Couples are able to work out

---

8. For a deeper discussion of these texts see: Clark, *Emerging Elders*, 84–91.

their disagreements, show love, and respect so that the children know "Mom and Dad love each other—therefore we are OK."

This is extremely important in blended families. Parent and stepparent must work together to help the children stay children. While the relationship may be different due to the presence of "ex-spouses," multiple visitation appointments, and other parents offering input, the spousal system must prevent the children from crossing their boundaries. The best thing the couple can do is to stay united, grow closer in their love, and support each other's addressing the children's behavior.

The second group is the sibling system. This system involves the children's relationships with each other. Those of us with children know that kids work together in this system. They have a relationship that will also last forever, even when they leave home. Parents might help to guide siblings to develop this relationship, but it does not have the same intimacy as that of the parents.[9] Parents can relate to their children and develop unique relationships with each, but it is much different from what couples offer each other. When children offer this love, support, respect, and encouragement parents are able to know "the kids love each other—we are OK."

In blended and adoptive families, siblings must be encouraged to develop their own relationships. Jealousy will always be present concerning step/adoptive children and biological children. It is a natural and normal occurrence. However parents must work together to teach the children that love and respect flow from the parents. As they model a healthy relationship, the children will sense this and learn how to love and respect each other. They will also have a sense of security knowing that "Mom/Dad and Stepmom/dad love each other—we are OK."

When the couple loves each other and has a healthy relationship the children can grow and develop normally. Couples who have strong relationships are able to work as a team to address issues and problems between children. Couples who love each other and stand together illustrate to the children that they are a team and cannot be manipulated. Children also learn that they can be

---

9. Balswick and Balswick, *Family*, 36–40.

children and do what children do. Children also feel safe because they see that their parents or stepparents love each other.

When the couple's relationship is stressed, lacks trust and intimacy, or becomes unhealthy children begin to feel anxiety.[10] Sometimes when parents stop communicating one puts that emotional energy toward one of the children. This is called triangulation and a triangle is formed that draws the child into the parental relationship. Relationships can form only along one axis, but in triangulation the child is caught between the parents.[11] Mother and father communicate through the child placing their anxiety on the child which can contribute to the child become a "little adult" and at risk for adult behavior (which becomes at-risk behavior). This is unfair to the child and the parents. Children need to worry about children's issues, not the adult's. Many times children who are in one of these triangles begin to act out and practice adult at-risk behaviors, confront the other parents, or try to parent the other siblings. This increases the anxiety to a family system and has a negative effect on the family.

Family-systems theory (FST) suggests that the family is a system or group that seeks equilibrium. The family members form an emotional unit.[12] As an emotional unit each member places an emphasis on shared responsibility, reciprocity, and repetition.[13] Rather than the unit being solely biological, it is mostly emotional. Members of the family live together and try to maintain balance or Shalom in the system. FST "emphasizes the function an individual's behavior has in the broader context of the relationship process."[14] Children and parents can create safe and sacred environments by working as a team to develop love, compassion, respect, and intimacy in their relationships. This

---

10. Becvar and Becvar, *Family Therapy*, 9–11; Gilbert, *Eight Concepts*, 7, 9; Kerr and Bowen, *Family Evaluation*, 7–8.
11. Cloud et al., *Unlocking Your Family Patterns*, 78.
12. Kerr and Bowen, *Family Evaluation*, 7.
13. Becvar and Becvar, *Family Therapy*, 9.
14. Kerr and Bowen, *Family Evaluation*, 48–49.

allows children to learn that relationships can be healthy while being alone offers time to develop oneself. This is individuation.

Conclusion

Families are to be enjoyed. A sacred family system allows children to develop and mature in a safe environment. Parents can create this sacred system intentionally, by being present, and encouraging individuation. Couples who love, support, nurture, and care for their relationship with each other and Jesus offer their children a chance to feel accepted and loved. This requires that parents think as spouses and parents in their daily lives.

When we moved to Portland to work in ministry at a larger church, we had intentionally decided to enroll our children into the public school. Our church affiliation had a Christian school available, which many other church leaders in our congregation and other area congregations had placed their children. We had always expressed that whether people enrolled their children in public, private Christian, or home school; each parent had to do what they felt was best for their children. Sometimes we witnessed parents being critical of each other over their choices. We heard comments made that suggested those of us who were in the public school system didn't care about our children. (I had an elder tell me that putting my son in a public school was like putting him in the middle of a highway.) Sometimes the home school parents were made to feel bad for their choices. Other times we heard that public institutions were anti-God. The reality is that all of us as parents had to make our choices and our children reflected the sacred and safe environments with which they were raised. Parents needed to view the congregation as a place to affirm and support each other, especially those of us in leadership.

It is important to remember, as ministers, that not only did we provided an example of family leadership for our congregation—but we needed to provide a safe and supportive environment for our people to disagree and yet feel valued. When we planted Agape Church of Christ our goal was to create a safe space for all people.

Over the years our boys have witnessed people from all walks of life. Business professionals, professors, construction workers, men and women from prostitution, those struggling with addictions, city workers, law enforcement, social service providers, missionaries, homeless men and women, street kids, and college students have all been welcome at Agape. We have worked hard to create a community where people can come, worship, and if they wish, heal. Our boys have learned that if our anxiety is low, the community will respond in that same way. They have not only observed us, but others who respond to a Shalom community. In turn, they have learned to be welcoming and act as leaders in their schools. Our hope is that the compassion we display in Portland and with our community, will be the same level of compassion they choose to show at school with various young boys and girls, as well as their teachers. This will in turn, give us a reason to enjoy the life that God has given us.

Discussion Questions

1. As a couple list some of the ways you can be intentional concerning your relationships.
2. How do you each wish to be "present" in your relationships and your future/current family system?
3. How is individuation "different" from "dependence"?

7

Adding a Leaf

> If you consider me a believer in the Lord, come and stay at my house... (Acts 16:15)

ONE OF OUR FAVORITE stories in the Bible is the story of Lydia's conversion. This possibly single woman persuaded her whole household (children, slaves, extended family) to be baptized into Jesus when she heard a sermon from Paul and Barnabas. After they were baptized, she responded with the above quote, which expressed a theme Luke used throughout Acts; Christian spirituality is witnessed by the hospitality of Jesus' followers. For Luke, when people offered hospitality to the Jesus' mission team, they were expressing their faith and commitment. Something spiritual happens when a meal is shared with others. Even more, something spiritual occurs when we share a meal with those outside our family or immediate circle of friends.

We both learned hospitality from our families. Lori's practiced it because they saw it in their parents and it was an expression of their Christian faith. Ron's practiced it because it was an expression of his mother's faith and his father's commitment as a human being. The fact that our parents opened their tables to others became an example to us. We had practiced this pattern in our lives before we married, but it became something we did as a couple in ministry. We learned from older couples in our church, leaders in our community, and ministry families who had deeply impacted us in discipleship that this was an important part of not only being a church community but also being human. If it was difficult to open the home, we were often taken out to eat at a restaurant by couples. Our time in Memphis, while in graduate school, was also a time where we learned from our church that any time we met we could eat together. We often joked that the church song, "Till we meet again" could be changed to, "Till we eat again." Church potluck dinners, Sunday afternoon meals, and small group meetings around the table impressed upon us that hospitality was an important quality of our faith, friendships, and spirituality. We even had families crowd into our small trailer because this was what it meant to be a community.

As a family we not only experienced joy around the table, we realized that we had to teach our children this concept. We made sure that our table always had a leaf. This was a reminder that the table was not just for our family, but for others as well. Our children have learned that people are welcome in our homes and that there will be nights each month where we will have guests. As our older son and his wife have lived in apartments we have heard their stories of inviting people to their homes and sharing food at the table. Hospitality is an important quality that children should learn.

Hospitality Teaches Grace and Faith

We live in a country where eating disorders abound. Most of these disorders involve anxiety, fear, and low self-esteem. While we admit that individuals who struggle with eating disorders have clinically diagnosed conditions, we understand that anxiety and control is a major part of these issues. Sometimes refusing to eat illustrates to others that one has control over their body—even if over nothing else in their lives. Our media explodes with weight-loss commercials, dieting advertisements, and health and body-image programs. We hear that America is grossly overweight, yet we also forget that our country also has some of the highest rates of anorexia, bulimia, and other eating disorders. While we admit that a healthy lifestyle is important in our daily activities, the reality is that food should express joy. Our media suggests that larger body size is now compared to a lack of discipline, laziness, low self-esteem, and now—an inability to be a good parent.

We control food portions in our public schools, yet remove active sports and the arts from our students' curriculum. We count calories, but do not count the rising financial cost of joining organized sports or renting musical instruments. We claim to be an overweight country but neglect the fact that so many children live in poverty and do not have sufficient food for the day. In the end, we fear the very thing God gave us to enjoy. With the church's invention of "gluttony" we struggle between a God who blesses feasting and a Savior who gathers leftovers with a religion that lists excessive eating as a "deadly sin." Even more the fashion industry has effectively limited female body size and helped us judge women by their waist, breasts, and posture. Why would we want to invite someone into our home to eat a meal around our tables?

Hospitality provides an opportunity to teach grace, faith, and sharing to our children and others. What better act of grace than to purchase extra food, eagerly prepare it, and serve it to someone without expecting a tip or financial compensation? What an opportunity to hold hands with people who may or may not have the same faith as we, and offer a prayer of thanks to the Creator! What an opportunity to teach our children that we will pay more and eat more today, believing that God will provide tomorrow! What an opportunity to show our children that serving people, whether they thank us or not, is a powerful testimony of our faith and who we are as humans. Because we interpret 1 Corinthians 11 as a challenge to the church concerning their taking communion while neglecting other members (like Corinthian slaves) who were without food, Agape offers breakfast in the mornings before worship for our guests who come from the street as well as those attending.

This form of hospitality brings rich and poor together. For Paul this was the true "Lord's Supper" or "Communion." Hospitality is an opportunity to practice faith and grace to others.

We have mentioned that blended families and adoptive families are an important part of this book. This is because both families practice hospitality. What better way to open your home, table, and relationships to another than to adopt a child. Blended families also offer this wonderful blessing. Children have the opportunity to have two sets of parents and extended brothers and sisters. While both families must work hard to grow and develop, they also are strong models of hospitality. We have been blessed to know wonderful loving families who adopt a child from another country, accept foster children, or raise children for their family or another local mother in the community. We have witnessed blended families fully participate in their children's sporting events, sit together, and peacefully support their children and stepchildren. While this is extremely difficult we have been encouraged to see this type of love, hospitality, grace, and acceptance that few individuals can offer. If families and children are willing to put away the perceived guilt and shame and recognize this as an opportunity to live out the Gospel of Jesus, families and all can be blessed through knowing these men, women, and children.

Hospitality Invites Others Into Our Lives

When we invite guests to our table we invite them to join us in our "ups" and "downs" for the day. There has always been a conversation around our table with our guests. Sometimes we just visit and eat together. Other times we talk about strategy, leadership plans, theology, biblical stories, current events, or do some counseling. However, during this time people's stories are shared. Lives are expressed. Guests talk to the children, the children answer back and learn to engage adults in conversation. We listen to stories as a whole, and many times we all find humor in them. The table can be filled with laughter and many times someone reluctant to laugh joins with us. The table is a place where we enter into each other's lives—and we feel a little closer after it is over. Even when someone we barely know joins us, the conversation is never awkward. If you don't want to talk, you can eat! If, or maybe when, you want to talk you are welcome to join in.

At Agape we also witness our members interacting over breakfast with those who are without food. They talk together, pray together, ask how each is doing, attend to needs, and make sure people are fed. Sometimes it's a huge spread of food, many times by those who struggle to provide for their own families at home. Other times there is just enough. Even more it is interesting that during worship and the sermon we can hear prayers, visiting, and attending to the needs of others happening simultaneously. It is a reminder that many times hospitality overrides the sermon!

One of the difficulties with ministry was that our children did not have the opportunity to "pick to be in ministry." What we mean is that our boys entered a family that embraced this calling, career, and way of life. While Nathan had a positive voice when we were discussing leaving an established church to plant Agape, our boys have understood that things such as going to church on Sundays, being in a small group, and accompanying us to do ministry was part of being in our family. When they leave home they can make their own decisions, but while they live with us, Jesus is Lord of our home and lives. Our boys have had to be with us when we visited nursing homes, handed out cheeseburgers to those on the streets, or talk to those we invited to our homes. They have had to be part of church work days, setup crews, and cleaning up at times. While we have always made it a point to make sure they aren't becoming "slaves" for the much needed work that has to be done, they know that they are expected to help in ways that they can. They have accompanied us into dark places and light places—yet we remind them that God is there. Our goal is for them to see that ministry does good to others and manifests courage, conviction, passion, and mercy.

They also know that mom and dad will never ask them to do what they will not do. In ministry, we have done things that are physically exhausting, mentally draining, and sometimes sickening. However, this is what it means to be a follower of Christ and they have come to expect to be involved. Inviting people into one's life and learning to love others is hard, but children can and need to learn this.

As boys growing up in a time, and in schools, where cultural masculinity is very strong, we have expected them to show compassion and grace, as well as courage to support their convictions. We know from our work with abuse, sexual assault, prostitution, gendered violence, and misogyny that males who lack "empathy" comprise the largest number of offenders in these crimes against humanity and sins against God. We also understand that empathy, compassion, mercy, and love are "ethical traits" that have to be taught to boys from both males and females. Yet we found that planting a church has taught them to offer love in the darkest corners of life, and challenge their friends who are judgmental toward those struggling with addictions, fighting poverty, living in dysfunctional families, and trying to balance the drama of life with peace and safety. It has also helped them to understand and be patient with those at their school who feel marginalized and neglected, which includes teachers as well as students. They are expected to be positive witnesses of our faith within their communities. The bottom line is that we wanted them to be part of something bigger than themselves, or us. To serve God is a noble calling for all of us, especially our children. However, they must see it first in their parents. This is especially true with young boys, as their need to trust others is enhanced by their relationships and view of themselves as part of something bigger than them.[1]

Hospitality Provides Boundaries and A Safe Space

At the table, if people choose not to talk, they can eat. Those who are shy typically listen while those who are more open to talking do (sometimes with a mouth full of food). Etiquette doesn't reign at our table, especially when someone laughs hard enough to have

---

1. Dykstra, Cole, and Capps, *Losers*, 7–8; idem., *Faith and Friendships*, 8.

their drink seep out of their nose—which causes more laughter to erupt. We aren't there just to be nice, we are there to be friendly and welcoming. At Agape we see a similar response to hospitality. Some talk, some ask to have demons removed, some visit and listen, some ask for prayer, some sleep, and some just wish to be left alone. It is a safe place to be who you want to be and eat what you want.

Boundaries are also an important part of hospitality. While Lydia opened her home to Paul and Barnabas in the book of Acts, many times we forget that who we invite sends a message to our children. There have been times when someone came to our home under the influence of alcohol or drugs, and one of us met them at the door and shared with them that they could not come over unless they were sober. There have been times when we have invited people to dinner but not to live in our home. There have been times when an emergency happened that we allowed someone to stay the night. There have been people in need who we asked to join us for a meal. Our boys saw this and understood what was happening.

First, they learned that our home was safe, sacred, and a place of refuge for them. We have heard too many stories of children sexually assaulted by a long-term guest, family member, college student residing in the home, or individual pushing the boundaries to stay in a home. We have heard the stories of parents allowing their children to move back home, only to wish for them to leave after years of residing with them. We do not want our boys, and others, to avoid coming to our house, their room, or dinner. We do not want our boys to see the home as a dangerous place with awful memories. We do not want to hear from our boys that we did not try to protect them (intentionally or unintentionally). We want our boys to be able to come home, feel safe, have their privacy, and be able to talk with us about their day or lives. We want our boys and their families to come home to visit and feel relaxed and at peace in their/our home.

Likewise we want to have a home where we as a couple can have our private time and unwind after work. We want to have a home where we can sometimes eat a meal in our pajamas and watch television. Sometimes when the boys spend the night at their friends' we love having the house to ourselves. Other times we love having their friends spend the night. Even more, we enjoy meeting at home alone for lunch and spending extra time in the quiet house. We have often encouraged our interns and ministry staff who move to Portland to not rent a place with others as we all need a time to come home and be alone to recuperate. This margin of peace is important for all individuals and families.

> Chronic busyness plagues most marriages and families today. No room exists in people's daily schedules for reflection, solitude, assessment, prayer, quality conversation, and other things that require stillness and focus. These crucial means of nurturing relationships are devalued and displaced by an endless stream of activities. Most families spend their days rushing from place to place. With technology and mass media feeding the insatiable thirst to be busy, more and more people lead a compulsive, activity-based existence.[2]

We read that at times Jesus sought to be alone with his disciples and family in his home, in the open, and at solitary places. People also need a safe place to escape and unwind.

While this might sound selfish, it is what we believe a home is meant to be. Some have people constantly present in their homes and spend little time as a couple in quiet, solitude, or eating with each other. Some people use the home as a pit stop on the way to a busy weekly schedule. Others see the home as a place too big to manage. However, the home should be a place that offers space for us to remove the busyness from our lives.

> In contrast, learning to place adequate and appropriate margins (time and space intentionally set aside to assess growth) around your marriage will dramatically contribute to its health and well-being. Overbooking your lives will make your marriage and family a much easier target for division. Building margins into your marriage means you give yourself permission to check out from the

---

2. Bragg and Bragg, *Marriage on the Mend*, location 2563.

obligations and responsibilities of everyday living and check in with each other in the areas that matter most.[3]

We view the home as a place to have Shalom or peace and Sabbath rest. We often comment that no matter how many rooms we have, our boys are sitting with us, on the couch, and in front of our television. We may all be using our smartphones, but we are in the same room. Other times wherever we go to visit, the boys come in to talk. Sometimes we would like more privacy or more rooms, but we realize that our home has its most important elements—the dinner table and us. Even more there are times when the boys choose not to go out with friends, and come home for the evening. We have often made the decision to say that they have been gone many nights and maybe they should stay home, which surprisingly is met with "OK, thanks." Then we have dinner together. Since our oldest son and his wife moved back to Portland we have noticed that our weekly family nights becomes a time when we eat dinner and hang out in the living room. We find that if our family is comfortable being at home, sometimes, then we have done our job. We are called to create a home that is a sacred/safe space. That seems to be a life of spirituality which happens with boundaries or margins in our lives.

During the summers we include youth groups and other organizations that join us to serve and work during our annual Agape Blitz which provides labor for schools, nonprofits, and other shelter or homeless camps. We invite the groups to our home for dinner, games, and to hang out for an evening. While there will many times be a large crowd we hear comments such as "comfortable," "normal," "peaceful," "relaxing," "inviting," while people are with us. It is a reminder to us that homes are not just safe and sacred places for our family, but others as well.

---

3. Ibid., location 2597.

Conclusion

If our children have a safe place at the table, then they should be able to go anywhere with good memories of their family, home, and hospitality. The table will continue to be a place for our grown children, and possibly their children, to gather and feel safe. We have listened to adult children of dysfunctional or abusive families share their anxiety concerning visiting for holidays or family gatherings. Some share that family members have to be intoxicated just to stomach the presence of other family members around the table. Others quickly eat and leave. Some respond to the stress by criticizing their own families or arguing with other members. Others simply choose not to attend. This is a tragedy. What was designed to be a place of joy, spirituality, hospitality, and love has become a place of tension, anxiety, and stress.

The marriage table can be a safe place where stories are told, retold, and. It can be a space where friends join us for holiday dinners (and maybe they witness healthy families). It can help those in romantic relationships see what their future might hold. It can become a powerful witness to the love of family sharing food, dreams, and stories.

Few remember what these tables look like, but they do remember what these tables provide.

Discussion Questions

1. How is hospitality a biblical concept?
2. What ways do you, or can you, begin to practice hospitality in your home?
3. Why are boundaries important in practicing hospitality?

8

Do We Need a Bigger Table?

For two years Paul stayed in his own rented apartment and showed hospitality to all who came to see him . . . (Acts 28:30)

HAVE YOU HEARD THE story of the witch, drug addict, former felon, prostitute couple, and family who played Trivial Pursuit one Thanksgiving? Probably not! However, it is a wonderful story and a true event. We have typically reserved Thanksgiving dinner for those in our church who do not have family. This one year we had many of our people join us, some who were mentioned above. We had an amazing time that evening, and our boys developed relationships with people who few will ever meet, let alone celebrate a holiday with. In the end, the couple who were sold into prostitution as teens, later met, and married won every game. We were all surprised they knew so much concerning trivia, the decades from the 1960s until the present, and life in general. One guest later told us, "I actually woke up the next morning and remembered the whole night." We joked with the witch/psychic who kept getting her answers wrong. Lori once exclaimed, "You're a psychic—I thought you would know all these answers." She exclaimed, "Well, now you know why I'm not rich."

While the day was fun, it was filled with many memories—even among our boys. They learned that people who are labelled as "deviant" in our society are not only worth loving but incredibly beautiful people. In the safety of our home, these men and women were able to play games with our children and find acceptance around the table. It has been a standard every year in our home that at Thanksgiving, we include many people for the day.

At our Christmas service we celebrated the baptisms of some of our guests. While it had been a Thanksgiving without fancy china or decorations, it was one that our family and friends will remember for years. Sometimes in the simplicity of a meal and open table, powerful stories are shared and experienced.

Our tradition also includes Christmas. While Thanksgiving is an open invite to many people, Christmas is a time when we focus on our family. We believe that our children not only need to learn to be hospitable with others, but they need to know that there are celebrations that we have with each other. Sometimes the crowded home is exciting, other times the small intimate gathering is just as important. Our boys know that in addition to making time for others, we provide time for them. They know that not only is the crowded home a sacrifice but the quiet personal time with us is as well.

A Great Missionary and a Small Apartment

The book of Acts ended in a surprising manner. The great Apostle Paul, traveled thousands of miles, baptized many men and women, established numerous churches, preached to thousands, and was one of the greatest influences of the Christian faith. He finally traveled to the great city of Rome, spoke to powerful dignitaries, and ended this spiritual ministry in a small apartment. At Rome he had a modest room paid out of his own money, which would have been located in one of the many crowded apartment complexes (called *insulae*) and had a rotating guard from the Roman army. Luke mentioned that he showed hospitality and preached to those who came to see him. Imagine this spiritual giant spending his last few years in a cheap apartment located in a crowded city and serving food to guests while talking about Jesus. While most apartment dwellers ate their meals in local restaurants, they still provided light food for guests in their apartments. It seems odd that this would be the end of the powerful story of the beginnings and growth of the early church. It seems odd that Luke would end Paul's story with his small meals, not his martyrdom. It seems so odd that some scholars feel that this is not the end of Luke's story—they suggest that he must have written another scroll.

Maybe the issue is not the ending. Maybe it is the fact that serving food in an apartment with a small group of people (and a Roman soldier) doesn't seem "sexy enough" to end this man's story. Maybe the problem was not Luke, or his scroll—maybe it is us. To believe that serving a meal, in the most meager of situations, with a small group of people can capture the qualities of our Christian movement takes faith. It, like hospitality, requires us to believe that small offerings bring great blessings.

Like Paul, we have witnessed the growth and joy that comes from open tables—no matter how small they are. We have witnessed many lives change through hospitality, intimate meals, and our family. After we were married we moved to a small town in Missouri, Bonne Terre, to preach at a very small church. The members were older and became grandparents to Nathan. He had wonderful adoptive grandparents as we began to see the church grow and develop children's classes, a youth group, and young married couple's classes. One of the women whom was especially fond of Nathan was a widowed lady named Laura Vureen. Nathan would go with us to visit her often and knew her very well. She had come to our home for holiday meals because her sisters lived in Texas and she had no family locally except for her church. When Nathan was five years old she contracted lung and brain cancer (she had never smoked a day in her life). Her face would light up when we would visit, even when she was weak from her chemotherapy treatment. The night that she was dying we were called to her side at one o'clock in the morning. We had to take Nathan with us as we didn't want to wake anyone to watch him. The nurses at the station offered to keep him while we went to pray and hold Laura Vureen's hand. As we were praying we saw Nathan in a wheelchair quickly pass by the door to her room. Lori quickly went out to get him only to find the nurses, one a member at our church, pushing him around the hall in the wheelchair. They had been feeding him chocolate cake for an hour and were cheering as they pushed him around the quiet ward. He was oblivious to Laura Vureen's struggles, but the nurses were having fun with him. Every time we would check on him he would be sitting with the nurses at a table eating or talking. Even in the midst of death and sorrow, joy continued through laughter around a table in a small breakroom.

We have taken our boys with us to do ministry, and they have met public officials, those sleeping in the streets, men and women in the sex industry, recovering addicts, missionaries, professors, ministers, business leaders, men and women suffering from sickness, college interns, police officers, abuse and trafficking advocates, and hospital and care facility patients. Most of these individuals have been in our home, and we have had a meal together. If our boys take anything away from these experiences, we hope that they see that the table is not a place to gobble down our food nor is it a prop in a family seeking to look successful. We hope that they see that the table is a place with history, memories, joy, and food. We hope that they remember more than what was served but who was served or serving. We hope that they see the table as a place to talk, share, and stay for a while. Even more we know that this is the key to healthy emotional and spiritual development.

Maturity develops when we begin to live in relationship and with others. For Agape we see this best practiced through hospitality. If we love, follow, and serve a Lord who ate with sinners we must not only teach but practice this for our children and others.

Do We Need a Bigger Table?

Putting Our Faith, Family, and Future to Practice

In 2006 we had been preaching at a large church in a suburb of Portland for eight years. It seemed like the natural progression to stay put, accept the salary, and try to help the church grow bigger. However God had called us to something else. When we resigned to plant a new church in downtown Portland we had no financial backing, no building, and only eight people willing to join us. We were not sure exactly where in Portland we would begin this new church. We had recently completed a one-week intensive church-plant evaluation and training to see if we were gifted to do this new work. During that week, near Seattle and during a February ice storm, the electricity to the cabin went out, our two little ones had stomach viruses, and it was below freezing. Ron was ready to go home, but Lori indicated that we should try to stick it out. Things got better and we passed the evaluations. Through time God provided funding, people, training, and support from the community. We saw firsthand that God provides for those who will embrace the vision to reach people. We knew that God had called us to this new ministry. God had already called us to ministry and we knew, as a family, that we would be faithful until we died.

It has not always been easy, but we have always been at peace. Our boys have done well in school and we continue to trust that God provides. We are ministering to some of the most difficult people, but our home continues to have a safe and sacred nature around the table. Our church also continues to attract men and women who also have this heart for others in our community. Our boys know that Mom and Dad love Jesus and each other passionately. They also know that we love them and are intentional about making time for their lives. It is hard, but the table offers a place of refuge and hope. As with the Apostle Paul the peace of God is sometimes understood in a small apartment, with a little preacher serving food to those who come to hear his message. It's not always important to have the biggest, flashiest, most expensive table—it's important to have one that is open, inviting, and welcoming.

As with the Apostle Paul, the culmination of all that Jesus has taught us may be best served at the family table, and one that reflects a marriage relationship that promotes Shalom, Sabbath, safety, and the sacred nature of God.

This is what it means to understand the safe and sacred way of Jesus.

Discussion Questions

1. What is odd about the way the book of Acts ends?
2. How does Paul's example offer us a deeper look into Christian hospitality?
3. What are some challenges that this ending offers to you?

Conclusion

May We Be Excused?

THANK YOU FOR JOINING us at this table, our metaphor of marriage. While we often hear about the "marriage bed," or "marriage vows," or "institution of marriage," it is good to find a different metaphor. The marriage table is something that is sacred, spiritual, and loving. The marriage table is safe, inviting, and offers good memories. The marriage table can glow with the warmth of good food and good conversation. The marriage table can be a place where people long to return and stay to visit long after the dessert is put away and the coffee cold. The marriage table can be a place where children speak and even the pickiest of eaters resides for hours. The marriage table can be a table for two, or one with a leaf. Sometimes when one eats by themselves, the prayer and table memories remind them that they are not truly alone. The marriage table can remind us of why we married and how we can please each other. The marriage table can be a place that is unplugged, uninhibited, and always understood.

Our conversation has ended, for now. We thank you for joining us at our table, and we hope you will also continue this story at your own table. Maybe you have come to realize that there is drama, pain, silence, awkwardness, or difficulty at your table. No matter what you cook, the tension is there. May we suggest that you see the table as more than a wooden structure that holds your plates, but a history that holds your hearts, your dreams, and your time? Maybe it's time to sit for a while at your tables and embrace this symbol of love and hope that can exist in all families. It is no coincidence that God not only joins us in a meal, but eagerly wants to be there.

> Moses and Aaron, Nadab and Abihu, and the seventy elders of Israel went up and saw the God of Israel, under whose feet was a pavement made of sapphire, clear like the sky. God did not raise a hand against the sons of Israel; they saw God, they ate, and they drank. (Exod 24:9–11)
>
> I passionately desire to eat this Passover meal with you before I suffer. (Luke 22:15)

If God wants to eat with us, and eagerly desires it, maybe it's time for us to eat together and give thanks for the Lord's blessings. May we please be excused?

Bibliography

Balswick, Jack O., and Judith K. Balswick. *The Family: A Christian Perspective on the Contemporary Home.* Grand Rapids: Baker, 1991.

Balswick, Jack O., Pamela Ebstyne King, and Kevin S. Reimer. *The Reciprocating Self: Human Development in Theological Perspective.* Downers Grove, IL: InterVarsity, 2005.

Becvar, Dorothy Stroh, and Raphael J. Becvar. *Family Therapy: A Systemic Integration.* 2nd ed. Boston: Allyn and Bacon, 1993.

Bergler, Thomas E. *The Juvenalization of American Christianity.* Grand Rapids: Eerdmans, 2012.

Bragg, Clint, and Penny A. Bragg. *Marriage on the Mend: Healing Your Relationship After Crisis, Separation, and Divorce.* Grand Rapids: Kregal, 2015. Kindle edition.

Cahill, Lisa Sowle. *Family: A Christian Social Perspective.* Minneapolis: Fortress, 2000.

Chapman, Gary. *Five Signs of a Functional Family.* Chicago: Northfield, 1997.

———. *The Four Seasons of Marriage: Secrets to a Lasting Marriage.* Carol Stream, IL: Tyndale, 2005. Kindle edition.

Clark, Ronald R. *Am I Sleeping With the Enemy? Males and Females in the Image of God.* Eugene, OR: Cascade, 2010.

———. *The Better Way: The Church of Agape in Emerging Corinth.* Eugene, OR: Resource, 2010.

———. *Emerging Elders: Developing Shepherds in God's Image.* Abilene: Abilene Christian University Press, 2006.

———. "Family Management or Involvement? Paul's use of *Prohistemi* in 1 Timothy 3 as a Requirement for Church Leadership." *Stone-Campbell Journal* 90 (Fall 2006) 243–52.

———. *Freeing the Oppressed: A Call to the Church Concerning Domestic Abuse.* Eugene, OR: Cascade, 2009.

Cloud, Henry, John Townsend, Dave Carder, and Earl Henslin. *Unlocking Your Family Patterns.* 3rd ed. Chicago: Moody, 2011.

Bibliography

Dunn, Richard R., and Jana L. Sundane. *Shaping the Journey of Emerging Adults: Life-Giving Rhythms for Spiritual Transformation.* Downers Grove, IL: InterVarsity, 2012.

Dykstra, Robert C., Allan Hugh Cole Jr., and Donald Capps. *The Faith and Friendships of Teenage Boys.* Louisville: Westminster John Knox, 2012.

———. *Losers, Loners, and Rebels: The Spiritual Struggle of Boys.* Louisville: Westminster John Knox, 2007.

Gilbert, Roberta M. *The Eight Concepts of Bowen Theory: A New Way of Thinking About the Individual and the Group.* Front Royal, VA: Leading Systems, 2006.

Gottman, John, and Nan Silver. *Seven Principles for Making Marriage Work.* New York: Harmony, 1999.

———. *What Makes Love Last? How to Build Trust and Avoid Betrayal.* New York: Simon and Schuster, 2012.

Hendrix, Harville, and Helen Lakelly Hunt. *A New Way to Love: Living God's Purpose for Your Marriage.* N.p.: CASP, 2009.

Kerr, Michael E., and Murray Bowen. *Family Evaluation.* New York: W. W. Norton, 1988.

Real, Terrence. *How Can I Get Through to You? Closing the Intimacy Gap Between Men and Women.* New York: Fireside, 2002.

Richardson, Ronald W. *Creating a Healthier Church: Family Systems Theory, Leadership and the Congregational Life.* Louisville: Fortress, 1996.

Sell, Charles M. *Transitions Through Adult Life.* Grand Rapids: Zondervan, 1991.

Sells, James N., and Mark A. Yarhouse. *Counseling Couples in Conflict.* Downers Grove, IL: InterVarsity, 2010.

Struthers, William M. *Wired for Intimacy: How Pornography Hijacks the Male Brain.* Downers Grove, IL: InterVarsity, 2010.

TenElshof, Judith K., and James L. Furrow. "The Role of Secure Attachment in Predicting Spiritual Maturity of Students at a Conservative Seminary." *Journal of Psychology and Theology* 28/2 (Summer 2000) 99–108.